Jacques Offenbach

**Offenbach in America:**

Notes of a travelling musician

Jacques Offenbach

**Offenbach in America:**
*Notes of a travelling musician*

ISBN/EAN: 9783337716059

Printed in Europe, USA, Canada, Australia, Japan

Cover: Foto ©Thomas Meinert / pixelio.de

More available books at **www.hansebooks.com**

# OFFENBACH IN AMERICA.

## NOTES OF A TRAVELLING MUSICIAN.

### By JACQUES OFFENBACH.

*WITH A BIOGRAPHICAL PREFACE*
By ALBERT WOLFF.

*Translated from advance sheets of the original Paris Edition.*

NEW YORK:
*G. W. Carleton & Co., Publishers.*
PARIS: C. LEVY.
MDCCCLXXVII.

COPYRIGHT, 1877, BY
G. W. CARLETON & CO.

JOHN F. TROW & SON,
PRINTERS AND BOOKBINDERS,
205-213 *East 12th Street*,
NEW YORK.

**THE**

# TO MY WIFE.

DEAR FRIEND.

It was you who wished me to make up a book from the scattered notes and random utterances of my heart. It is the first sorrow you have caused me. I bear you so little grudge, however, that I beg you will allow me to dedicate this volume to you, not for what it contains or for what it is worth, but because I love to manifest in every way my esteem and my affection for you.

JACQUES OFFENBACH.

# CONTENTS.

|  | PAGE |
|---|---|
| BIOGRAPHICAL PREFACE, BY ALBERT WOLFF | 7 |

### CHAPTER I.
Before Leaving................................. 35

### CHAPTER II.
The Passage Out................................ 43

### CHAPTER III.
New York—Gilmore's Garden..................... 54

### CHAPTER IV.
The Houses—The Streets—The Cars.............. 61

### CHAPTER V.
Theatres in New York........................... 68

### CHAPTER VI.
Art in America................................. 79

### CHAPTER VII.
Restaurants—Three Types of Waiters............ 85

### CHAPTER VIII.
American Women—Introductions—Central Park.... 95

### CHAPTER IX.
The Story of Two Statues....................... 100

### CHAPTER X.
Liberty in America............................. 109

### CHAPTER XI.
Societies and Processions...................... 121

## CONTENTS.

| | PAGE |
|---|---|
| CHAPTER XII. | |
| Advertising and Puffing | 123 |
| CHAPTER XIII. | |
| The Turf—Jerome Park | 128 |
| CHAPTER XIV. | |
| The American Newspaper Press | 132 |
| CHAPTER XV. | |
| A Few Character Sketches | 141 |
| CHAPTER XVI. | |
| Philadelphia | 153 |
| CHAPTER XVII. | |
| Offenbach Garden | 157 |
| CHAPTER XVIII. | |
| On the Way to Niagara—Pullman Cars | 161 |
| CHAPTER XIX. | |
| Niagara Falls | 166 |
| CHAPTER XX. | |
| The Dauphin Eleazar | 169 |
| CHAPTER XXI. | |
| Return from Niagara—Sleeping Cars | 172 |
| CHAPTER XXII. | |
| The Miseries of a Musician | 180 |
| CHAPTER XXIII. | |
| The Firemen of New York | 187 |
| CHAPTER XXIV. | |
| Banquets, Baton, and Brevet | 198 |
| CHAPTER XXV. | |
| Farewell Night | 205 |
| CHAPTER XXVI. | |
| Homeward-Bound | 207 |

# BIOGRAPHICAL INTRODUCTION.

### By ALBERT WOLFF.

---

*To Madame* HERMINIE OFFENBACH:

MADAME—Your husband's publisher has requested me to write a preface to this book, which he has dedicated to you. It was not necessary that your name should appear on the first page, for us to be convinced that you were worthy of every proof of affection and gratitude. Whatever your husband writes, whether music or words, belongs to you by right. There is not a single one among your innumerable friends but is aware that you are not only the best of wives, and the most excellent of mothers, but that also, and to a certain extent, you have participated in the works signed by our illustrious composer.

The numerous productions of your husband

may be divided into two quite distinct parts: the one is like the echo of Parisian gossip, Boulevard bustle, and artistes' suppers, when French mirth and good humor have been stimulated by sparkling champagne; the other part has nothing in common with the first, and is your legitimate property, for it is you, Madame, who have blessed this thoroughly Parisian artiste with a happy and genial home, where his heart has expanded at ease in the midst of a charming, joyful, and spirited family, where he has most unquestionably found the pathetic and more delicate tones of his repertory, which, in my humble opinion, form the purest part of his talent. This is why I think of your husband when the blasts of frolicking mirth burst forth in his music, and I think of you, Madame, when suddenly, through the jingling bells of folly, plaintive melodies glide out harmoniously, and delight the ears both of connoisseur and crowd. Quite lately, Madame, I was staying a few hours in the ancient city of Cologne, and chanced to pass before the house where your husband was born. Jacques was already a well-grown youth, and something of a virtuoso, when I was learning to read in the school adjoining his father's house. None better than I can tell you of his start in life, for the Offenbach family form one of the earliest memories of my childhood; I knew the parents of Jacques, his brothers and his sisters, who certainly did not at that time suspect that the fair-haired boy, who was so fond of his violoncello, would become the most popular musician of his time, and that the little lad, who bid them good-morning every day as he went past, would one day write this preface.

The house in which Jacques was born was small. I see it still, on the right of the courtyard, at the farthest end of which my school was situated. The front door was low and narrow; the kitchen, clean and bright, was located under the hall; copper saucepans hanging on the walls in beautiful order; the mother busy at her range; on the right, after crossing the kitchen, a sitting-room looking out on the street. The father reclining in his big arm-chair near the window, when not engaged giving music lessons; he had a good voice, and played on the violin. Mr. Offenbach was already an elderly man; I have preserved a two-fold remembrance of the good man: when, on leaving school, I made too much noise in the yard, he would come out and administer to me a gentle correction, and on holidays he would cram me with cakes, in the making of which Mother Offenbach had no rival in the town. There is no house where I have been oftener whipped and more spoilt, than in that of your late father-in-law.

Everybody in that house was more or less of a musician, from the father down to the youngest son, whom death carried off so early, and who was said to be gifted with much talent. The house in the Rue de la Cloche had a modest appearance; the family was a large one, and the father's income did not allow of excessive expenses. I was often told in my young days that Father Offenbach had to make the greatest sacrifices to enable his son Jacques to take music lessons.

I well remember your husband's professor, whom, in my childhood, I used to see sometimes in the streets, wearing a threadbare coat with brass buttons, the tails of which reached down to his calves, a cane with an ivory handle, a brown wig, and one of those broad-brimmed hats then in fashion. Despite his comparatively comfortable income, M. Alexander, the professor, was generally considered the greatest miser in the town. It was said that he had once exhibited great talent; and he was known in his own neighborhood by the glorious name of "the Artiste." It was of him that Jacques took lessons, at the rate of twenty-five cents each. The end of the month was generally a hard time for the Offenbach family; but they deprived themselves of many little comforts in order to economize the price of the lessons, for Herr Alexander did not trifle with such matters; the twenty-five cents had to be spread on the table before the beginning of the lesson. No money, no music!

This earliest and most accurate impression which I have preserved of Jacques' youth, coincides with the first visit he paid his parents on returning from Paris. It was an event for all the friends of the family, where, for a long time past, nothing had been talked of except Jacques, who, it was currently reported, was coining millions in Paris by playing on the violoncello. Nobody in Cologne suspected that the father of Offenbach's son earned his scanty living with great difficulty on the banks of the Seine. The mere fact that he was listened to in Paris, the city of artists and rich people, no one ever doubted but what Jacques must be a millionnaire. It was said in the town: "Father Offenbach is a lucky man; it appears that his son is coming back with big diamonds instead of buttons in his waistcoat, and that his fortune is reckoned by hundreds of thousands of francs."

It was not this which drew me to the Offenbachs'. In our youth we have but a very vague idea of wealth; a ten-cent piece or the vaults of the Bank of France seem about alike; but if, in the evening, at the hour at which Jacques was expected, I found myself among the friends of the house, it was because on the morning of the same day I had smelt the savory perfume of those famous cakes; I had been struck with astonishment at this extraordinary occurrence, for it was not the eve of a holiday. But, in reply to my eager inquiries, Mother Offenbach had replied: "This is a fête-day for us all, my boy; my son Jacques comes back this evening from Paris. Come in by and by, and have some cakes; I can tell you that I have spared neither eggs, nor butter, nor sugar."

When about sun-down I crossed the threshold of the house, in the Rue de la Cloche, Jacques, who was sitting on the sofa by the side of his father, whilst his mother was getting supper ready for the beloved son—Jacques, I repeat, was for me but an object of the greatest curiosity. But my heart beat faster as I caught sight of a bottle of Rhein-wine standing on the white table-cloth between two dishes filled with delicacies, the whole sparkling under the light of a small brass chandelier, which was only lighted on great occasions. At that moment there was not in the town a happier house than this. Relatives and friends came in one after another, to welcome Jacques; and each time a fresh visitor came in, the dishes were sent around, and each time I helped myself to some fresh delicacy, so that, as a natural consequence, a formidable fit of indigestion nailed me for a week to my bed; but I bear no grudge to your husband for all that, believe me, Madame!

I am quite sure that I did not then realize the influence which this visit was destined to have on my future life; but I think that it was then I unwittingly conceived the idea of going later to Paris, like young Offenbach, and of coming back, like him, to my family, made much of by everybody, and, in the absence of my father, whom I had hardly known, I beheld myself, in the distant future, sitting by the side of my mother, who looked as happy as Mother Offenbach. I could see the table groaning under the weight of cakes, and the rapture of my mother, as proud of her son as Mother Offenbach of hers. Alas! this greatest of joys, dream of my boyhood, I was never able to give to my poor mother, who died young, and who was also an excellent woman, like yourself, Madame.

If I dwell on this reminiscence of my youth, puerile to the indifferent, but which so greatly affects me when my thoughts travel back to those happy days, it is that you may know,

Madame, how Jacques' career became in some way closely connected with mine.

Later, when I came to Paris, and the Figaro consented to harbor my early efforts, the first person whom I met in the office of that journal was Jacques, and it was then that I began to reflect on that mysterious destiny which brings about the realization of a boyish dream, twenty years later, in the presence of the very man who first directed his mind towards the great city.

At this time Jacques was already a great man; he was no longer merely the talented violoncellist of former days; he had long since abandoned the little stage in the Champs Elysées, which was the cradle of his fame. The Bouffes Theatre was giving every night that *Orphée aux Enfers*, which has gone around the civilized world, and has contributed so much to establish his popularity. I had introduced myself to the celebrated composer, and he had deigned to put my name on the free list at the Bouffes. But the house was crowded every evening; my ticket really admitted me no farther than the lobby, and it was through the glass window of a box door that I saw the piece and heard the music. Now, Madame, that I have the honor of being your friend, and that I have the conviction of being sufficiently near your heart to be able to speak to you of my troubles, and my joys, you will allow me doubtless to say that the success of *Orphée* is in some degree the starting-point of this preface. At that time I was poor, and blushed when the usher rushed forward to take my overcoat. What could I do? I was obliged to be economical in order to breakfast the next day; everybody has not the means of giving ten cents to an usher. But when, sad and desperate, I walked the streets of Paris, gazing curiously at the stars, wondering what the future had in store for me, and gliding along close to the walls of the houses in order that those whom I met might not see my weakness, I always ended by finding myself at the Bouffes; I heard the applause of the public; I thought of the young Offenbach, who started so low in the social ladder, and who had raised himself so high; and I went home with a comforted mind and a better heart; I measured the distance between Father Offenbach's little house and that brilliant house where the public hailed so lustily your husband's music; and I thought within myself that, with some talent, a great deal of energy, and an enormous amount of work, I should never find myself under the necessity of returning to Cologne.

You see, Madame, that fate has taken pity on my anguish, since I have the good fortune to write you from Paris, where I have suffered so much, but to which I owe the little that I am, and which I love so much, that it seems impossible to me I could have been born elsewhere, just as it appears to me unaccountable that the incarnation of Parisian wit in music—that is, your husband—should be the same Jacques I once saw sitting by the side of his father in the little house in the Rue de la Cloche, at Cologne.

If I speak so much of myself, Madame, it is not to attempt to move your feelings on the subject of my past life, but to draw your attention to the strange coincidences of this life. As I have had the honor of telling you: I strayed the last time I travelled into the Rue de la Cloche, where your husband was born, and all these memories of former days came back to my mind. And I had hardly set foot again on the Paris pavement, before I learned that Jacques was about to publish a book on America. My good friend, Calmann Levy, asked me to write him, not a preface, but a few biographical notes on Jacques Offenbach. This will explain to you why I have been compelled to associate my name, which is simply a known one, with that of your husband, which is a famous one.

The old house in the Rue de la Cloche has ceased to exist, Madame. On the site where it formerly stood, a dazzling monument has been reared. Fair Jacques and the cottage of his ancestors have shared the same fate; they have both grown with time. The violoncello with which Jacques obtained his first successes was laid aside at the same time that the paternal cottage was pulled down. Jacques also is now a moving monument of Parisian music; and, if I use this term, it is not with a view of diminishing its value, but to indicate its leading characteristics—the wit and good humor of the great city in its moments of explosive mirth.

Here and there, with this eminently Parisian talent, you find mingled something like a pious reminiscence of the old home at Cologne. I do not think that Jacques is capable of looking long upon the humble portrait of his father, hung above his piano, without being moved by the memory of those happy days. In his hours of meditation, his thoughts must dwell on the old songs of his youth, and it is then that he drops upon paper those sweet and serene melodies which, to the utter astonishment of the public, suddenly appear in his works, and produce the unforeseen effect of a young girl, chaste and innocent, who, in the radiant simplicity of her beauty, clad in white, and with a single flower in her bosom, appears in the midst of a masked ball, where folly reigns supreme.

And it is precisely this sudden apparition of what I would term the homely muse of your husband which places his work far above the noisier part, which, by way of antithesis, might be called the muse of the boulevards. But this is also the secret of the marked success obtained by Jacques; his inexhaustible repertory is a combination of every kind of sentiment; the spirited strains that take the house by storm; the bluff laugh that pleases some; the Parisian wit that bewitches others; and the pathetic touch that makes all the world akin, because it springs from the heart and goes straight to the soul. Therein lies the secret of his brilliant successes and of that popularity which must have been witnessed at home in order to realize its extent. Nothing has been wanting to his long-lived triumph in a branch of art which people persist in calling small; but in the way of art, Madame, nothing is small. The *Song of Fortunio* is not written in five acts, and does not require the vast stage of the Opera; yet it is the complete gem of a composer in love with his art. The *Brigands* comprise exquisite passages which the big boots of the carabineers, imagined to please the crowd, are not able to stifle under the weight of their heavy tread. The *Sabre de mon Père* may be called in question, despite its loud success; but the most hardened purist in musical matters cannot deny that the *Dites lui*, in the *Duchesse de Gerolstein*, is a genuine pearl. Your husband's works,

Madame, swarm with such graceful and pathetic melodies; and it is surely on that account that he remains the colonel of the regiment of composers who have followed in the path marked out by Jacques.

I do not mean to imply by the above, Madame, that, outside of Jacques, opera bouffe does not exist. You are too intelligent to think that your husband has done all that can be imagined in the line he has created; he has given it a fair start, and that is a great deal; for a man can only be reckoned an artiste on condition of giving a personality to his art; and the art of Jacques is essentially the art of Jacques. Whether it be a more or less great art is not the question. In order to judge an artiste, it must be first ascertained whether his art is really his own, or whether he has learnt and borrowed it of others. It is said of some that they have brought this style to life again; of others that they resemble that man; but the whole is covered by the general expression: "Offenbach style," which is in everybody's mouth, and which gives your husband a share in the very success of his followers.

In Jacques' long career all has not been triumph and good luck; he has had to struggle, like everybody else. When a brain is full of such joyous and charming melodies, and its owner is obliged to act as leader to the orchestra of the *Théâtre Français* between the two acts of a tragedy, he is entitled to a place in the ranks of celebrated martyrs. Is it possible to conceive a more cruel torture than that of a richly endowed mind condemned to devote its energy to so humble and ungracious a task? Artistes are sometimes reproached with having an excessive veneration for their own talent; but what would they do without that faith in themselves which sustains them in the hour of trial? Is it possible to blame a man of talent, condemned to lead a wretched orchestra, with blowing his own trumpet, in order to keep alive the illusions which save him from the fatal consequences of a faint and sad heart.

Henri Heine, who had known every kind of suffering, wrote the following terrible truth:

" Adversity is a hideous old witch. She is not satisfied with paying us one visit; she sits by our bed, settles herself there with her work-box, and takes out her knitting like a person who intends making herself at home for some time!"

Well, Madame, in presence of this weird visitor, the artiste can only keep himself going by the consciousness of his value, and if, in the hour of triumph, painfully achieved, the mind, rid of this abominable nightmare, gives vent to a shout of joy, and chants a hymn to its own glory, who would dare to reproach it with an excess of pride, so dearly bought at the price of so much discouragement?

If anybody has the right to be proud of his success, it is surely your husband, Madame. You who have assisted him in this terrible struggle against fate, you know better than I what amount of courage and energy was required to overcome, one after the other, all the obstacles in his path. If Jacques has drunk deeply the cup of success, he began by making the acquaintances of all the miseries of adversity. Unable to find anybody to play his music, he was obliged to rent a theatre of his own, in order to place his own pieces on the stage; and when at last he contrived to open a small house in the Champs Elysées, and he might consider himself as having reached the goal of his ambition, the administration came down upon him with its shackles of red tape, and compelled him to restrict his intelligence to the narrow frame of pieces with only three characters. He was obliged to conquer step by step the ground on which he has erected the monument of his reputation, and I am not sure that without your encouragement and your attentions your husband would have finally triumphed. I am therefore right in saying, Madame, that you have participated in his works, and that this book belongs to you by right as much as the Maestro's scores.

I know, Madame, that, in the course of Jacques' long and active career, success has not always been spontaneous, and the public has often been unjust towards your husband. I persist, for instance, in considering the *Bergers* as one of his best scores, although it was not played hundreds of nights. It is also quite natural that amid so many triumphs, like the *Mariage aux Lanternes, la*

*Belle Hélène, la Grande Duchesse, la Vie Parisienne, les Brigands,* and a hundred other plays whose titles it is needless to enumerate, his talent should have been at times unequal. But in art, whether small or great, it is only mediocrity which has the privilege of being always at the same level of sufficient insufficiency. Investigating minds, ever anxious and agitated, do not know the never-disturbed joys of permanent satisfaction; they are one day at the summit and the next, if not at the bottom, at least at the middle of the ladder. Inspiration has its good and evil hours; the artiste lives on fits of elation and despair. It may be said that in Jacques' colossal repertory a few operettas are of comparatively small value, but of not one can it be said that it is worthless. In his least-prized works there is always to be found considerable talent and unquestionable individuality. It is always, and despite everything, an art which belongs to him personally, and a few distant chords suffice to leave no doubt as to the author. He is as easily recognized as a flower at night by its peculiar fragrance.

Nothing, Madame, has been wanting to complete the success of your husband. To the applause of the public in every country there has been added the disparagement of a few. But the last have never been able to stem the torrent of his success. Jacques has, for instance, been reproached with having, under another *régime*, contributed towards what was called the demoralization of the people—an empty and confused term, which looks as if it meant something, but which really specifies nothing—like all the nonsense talked by people who wish to give themselves an air of importance; this category of silly detractors has a whole assortment of old sores. As for myself, every time I meet a man who says to me: *Tu quoque Brutus?* or *Quousque tandem abutere patientia nostra?* I fight shy of him, for he is on the point of singing the eternal romance of the demoralization of the people by a theatrical piece.

It cannot, however, be denied, Madame, that part of your husband's work is a fair reflex of the period in which it was conceived, and it is moreover on that very account that Jacques' talent has its place marked in the history of this century. Indeed, in his greatest successes, of some twelve or fifteen years ago, there is still evident the Paris of those days—the merry, careless Paris, the Paris that loves to laugh, dance, and, in a word, to amuse itself. But how could he have become an artiste of his time, if he had not felt the commotions of his time? A man must belong to his age, in every branch of art, without exception. Such was Carpeaux; and for this very reason he has proved superior to all the sculptors who looked but on the past. What is it that endears to us the artistes of former times, whose work was modelled after the ideas of the period? Teniers, for instance, in the picture of a merry beer-drinker of his day, can much more rightly claim the name of historical painter than those of our contemporaries, who twice a week begin over again, *Cæsar before the Rubicon*, or else the *Battle of Pharsalia*. If, then, Jacques has really been the musician of his period, he has fulfilled his task, and more attention will be paid to his work than to the sterile efforts of those who have never done anything else than emulate what existed before they came into the world, and have worn out on the pavement of the boulevards what remained of the old shoes of the preceding generation.

And that is why the name of Jacques Offenbach is one of the most popular of the time and his talent has delighted the great majority of the public. When a work pleases at once connoisseurs and the crowd, its value is beyond dispute. Jacques is a modern man; his music has *le diable au corps*, like our busy century, rushing on under full head of steam. The finale of the first act of the *Brigands* could never have been conceived in the days when chaise and coach were the only means of locomotion. It is genuine nineteenth century music; the music of express-trains and screw-steamers—in a word, of the diabolical bustle of our time; and this is why it is popular, not only in France, where Jacques' talent has grown up and to which the composer belongs, but in every country; and I do not think there exists a musician more truly popular than your husband; and very certainly he will leave his children a name which will act for them as a passport in the four corners of the globe.

Suppose, Madame, that, some ten years hence, your young son should take it into his head to travel about the world. One fine day—do not be frightened, Madame; this is only a supposition—one fine day he falls into the hands of cannibals:

"Ah!" says the chief, "here is a young paleface, who would be very good eating with a bit of salad."

Then addressing his victim, he says:

"What is thy name, savory stranger?"

"I am the son of Jacques Offenbach."

"Cheer up, young man; thou wilt not be eaten!" exclaims the chief. "And now let the fun begin!" and immediately young Offenbach is hoisted onto a throne, the savages strike up the finale of *Orphée* in token of their joy, and it only depends on your son's inclination for him to become at once king of something or other, for all the world like Orélius, the Perigueux attorney.* This is what ought to give you good hope for the

* Orélie Antoine I., King of Auricania.

future, Madame. I have never paid a visit to the savages, but I am an incorrigible touriste. In all the countries where I have travelled the name of Jacques Offenbach is equally celebrated; and, believe me, a man who captivates to this extent the attention of his contemporaries is a man of worth, and it may be said of him that if ever in the future his talent should decay, what he has already produced has such a solid foundation that I defy Jacques ever to ruin his own reputation. Despite all criticism — and everybody has the right to criticise—there is one point upon which all are of the same way of thinking, namely, that his talent is unquestionable. Some have called him a vulgarizer; but this word, which, in the mouth of your husband's enemies, would imply censure, is the greatest praise which he could covet. It is not easy to vulgarize an art; that is to render the charm and seduction of music accessible to the refractory brains.

At this moment, Madame, your husband is about to make his first appearance in the field of literature. Nobody ever knows what will be the fate of a book; and I do not think that the publisher, in asking me for a preface, had the intention of setting me to study Offenbach as a writer of prose. This will explain why in this preface I have spoken to you of everything except of this book. The certain success of the work will be found on the title-page, which bears the popular name of the author. A little more or a little less literary merit would add nothing to Jacques' reputation as a musician, and would in no way diminish his reputation as a man of wit; but I should not be surprised if this literary fancy of a composer of great talent proved a great success as a selling book. All those who owe so many pleasant evenings to Jacques must be curious to know how he writes; they will find in the narrative of his travels in America the same cheerful ease, and the same spontaneous wit which they have been accustomed to find in his scores. Besides, I do not think that in writing these pages your husband had the intention of overthrowing the statue of Christopher Columbus and of placing himself in its stead on the quay of Geneva. Jacques cannot precisely be said to have discovered America, but he contributes a few personal ideas to all that has been written on the New World.

You, dear Madame, who are one of the most distinguished women I have met, you would not forgive me were I to say more. Your tact is so sure in all these things that I should surely lose your esteem if I were to state that French literature has just been enriched with a glorious monument. Moreover, it is not with the view of such a high destiny that Offenbach has jotted down in black and white his travelling impressions. It may be that the wind shall one of these days blow these light leaves away, but what is very sure is, that you and your children will keep them lovingly as a souvenir of that distant voyage undertaken by an artiste in weak health, under altogether special circumstances—not to seek fresh laurels, with which he could well dispense, but in order to fulfill the duty of an honorable man and of a family chief truly worthy of the name.

This book, Madame, will console you when you think of the sad days you spent during his long absence. Joy has returned to your house, for a time so silent and sad. I avail myself of this favorable disposition to ask you to excuse me if I have placed your name at the head of this preface without asking your leave. It has afforded me great satisfaction to address these lines to you in acknowledgment of the valued friendship with which you honor me. In this skeptical and busy city you have created a really artistic drawing-room, which is one of the curiosities of Paris, and at the same time a place of relaxation for those friends who, wearied by the feverish Parisian life, come to breathe at their ease the sweet and serene atmosphere of family life, honorable, laborious, and respected. In this charming home it is quite natural that your husband should have developed the more salient qualities of his talent: Wit and Elegance.

PARIS, January, 1877.

# OFFENBACH IN AMERICA

## CHAPTER I.

### BEFORE LEAVING.

Towards the end of the spring of 1875 I was occupying with my family one of the three large pavilions on the terrace of St. Germain. I am extremely fond of this admirable spot, and I had sought refuge there in the very pardonable hope of enjoying the rest which had become necessary after a most laborious winter.

My door had been closed against all strangers, and, above all, against all those who had a near or remote connection with theatrical affairs. Twenty years of work and struggle seemed to me sufficient to justify this harsh, but, you will admit, just measure.

I was thus living quietly in the midst of my family—a very numerous one—and of my intimate friends. It was not absolute solitude, but it was at least peace and quiet.

One morning, while I was playing in the garden with one of my children, Mademoiselle Schneider's visit was announced. I had not the heart to order the rules enforced against her; I have much friendship for the Grande Duchesse de Gerolstein, and, when I meet her, it always seems to me as if I saw my successes walking about.

We were chatting of everything and of nothing—of the great battles we had fought together before the footlights—and, why should I not say it, of our past victories, and perhaps also of the battles to come—when I was handed a card, on which I read a name completely unknown to me.

I was about scolding my servant, when the owner of the card made his appearance in person. He was a very correct and polite-looking gentleman; but I saw at once I had to deal with a man going straight to the point, and that, willing or not, I should be obliged to hear what he had to say; so I submitted to my fate.

"Pray, sir," he said to me, "excuse this intrusion upon your privacy, but I have come to see you on important business; I will not detain you long, for you will only have to answer yes or no."

"I am listening, sir."

"I am commissioned, sir, to ask you whether you would like to go to America?"

I was so little prepared for such a formidable proposition, that I could not help laughing right out.

"Let me assure you, sir," I said to my visitor, "that even for a large sum of money I would not go to St. Cloud to-day."

"I am not speaking of St. Cloud, or of to-day, sir. The simple question is, will you go to the Philadelphia Exhibition next spring?"

"To Philadelphia! and, pray, for what purpose?"

"Americans, sir, are very partial to great artistes; they welcome them magnificently, and pay them in the same style."

"Well, sir, I must confess that your proposal is a serious and very flattering one, and that at any rate it seems well worthy of consideration."

"Oh! sir, I never expected that you would decide on the spot. Take your own time. I have but a very simple mission to fulfil—to know whether you would like to go to Philadelphia. If you give me a favorable reply, the interested parties will come and confer with you; if not, I shall only regret having intruded upon you, while not forgetting the honor you have done me, in deigning to listen to what I had to say."

I remained silent for a moment: a thousand thoughts coursed through my brain. Those who have families, and who are conscious of their duty, will understand without explanation what these thoughts were; as for others, they would not understand them even with a lengthy explanation.

At last I replied:

"Well, sir, I cannot say that I would *like* to go to America, because, irrespective of my fifty years of age, there are many things which detain me here; however, in due time, and under such conditions as you lead me to expect, I should not hesitate to go."

My visitor bowed.

"This is all I wish to ascertain," he said.

During breakfast I spoke of the visit I had just received; but although my tale was told in the most jovial tone possible, it met with no success whatever.

"It is madness!" was the general outcry.

I hastened to demonstrate that the affair was in no wise to be taken in earnest; I even offered to bet that I should never hear any more of it. But a cloud had settled over the minds of all, my own included, and there it remained for the rest of the season. How little it takes to sadden happy days, and what folly it is to leave the front door open!

The very next day I received the visit of M. Bacquero, who had hastened to write as soon as he had heard of my decision.

M. Bacquero is a business man in the best meaning of the term; his offer was such that I did not think myself justified in hesitating an instant, and I at once signed the engagement which he tendered me.

On that day it was needless for me to relate what had occurred; my family had guessed the result of the visit, and I became more than ever aware, on seeing my wife and children making so many vain efforts to conceal their tears, of the sweet and holy affection with which I was surrounded. So much sadness and such gentle reproaches were not calculated to give me the courage of which I stood more in need than any one thought. I spent long, sleepless nights, and in the morning dared not go to sleep, lest on waking I should not be able to command a smile in order to comfort the dear souls who came to greet me with a sorrowful good-morning. Then I imagined a thousand tranquillizing theories. We had the winter before us—a winter is a very long period of time—who knows what may happen in the course of nine months? The Exhibition might not take place, or might be indefinitely postponed; such things occurred every day. America had had a long war; another might break out again—in fact, it was almost sure to do so. I was in the position of the poor devil in the fable whom the king had commanded to teach his ass to read, under penalty of being hanged. The good man had accepted, asking ten years to accomplish this miracle; and, as he was blamed, he replied:

"It would be bad luck, indeed, if in ten years either the king, the ass, or myself is not dead."

But the philosopher had ten years before him to accomplish this miracle, whereas I had only six months; the time seemed to pass with lightning speed.

One last hope remained—a very human, very prosaic hope. According to the terms of the agreement, a considerable sum of money was to be deposited in my friend Bischofsheim's bank, and I had endeavored to convince myself, in order to convince my family, that this formality would not be accomplished.

One day I met one of those men who always know all the news, nobody knows how; and, as soon as he caught sight of me, he exclaimed:

"I have heard from yonder; your funds will not come."

It seemed to me as if this amiable man had roused me in the middle of a frightful nightmare. Instead of going to the club, I told the coachman to drive back home, and the worthy fellow sent his horse along at a rattling pace, knowing full well that I was the bearer of good news.

Indeed, I had no sooner communicated the gossip, than everybody's face beamed with joy, and frantic delight took possession of the household. It did not last long, however. On the appointed day the cash was deposited; and this momentary delight only served to intensify the grievous sorrow of parting.

## CHAPTER II.

#### THE PASSAGE OUT.

The moment had come. Always a painful one for a man who has lived all his life in Europe, and who is about to enter upon a long journey towards a distant country; and it was only after long hesitation that I finally resolved to undertake the proposed voyage.

I left Paris on the 21st of April. My two sons-in-law, Charles Comte and Achille Tournal, my two brothers-in-law, Gaston and Robert Mitchel, and a few friends—among whom were Albert Wolff, Mendel, and my son—accompanied me to Havre. I was deeply moved when I went on board the ship the next morning. I had endeavored to make the separation less painful by leaving my wife and daughters in Paris; but how I regretted them now!

The ship started; and, as she grazed the pier,

and my eyes dwelt for the last time on my young boy, I felt a pang within, me such as none but a father can understand.

While the ship was steaming away, my eyes were riveted upon that little group, in the midst of which stood my dear child. The sun shining brightly on the brass buttons of his college uniform, enabled me for a long time to make out the exact spot where he stood, and which my heart would otherwise have guessed.

Here I am on the *Canada*, a fine ship, spick and span new.

She left the quay at eight o'clock in the morning, and we are already far from land. The vessel is a fast one. Like myself, she is making her first trip to America. Accustomed to first representations, I do not mind being present at her first appearance on the ocean.

Allow me now to introduce to you a few of the ship's company. *A tout Seigneur, tout honneur.*

Captain Franzeue is a true sailor, an excellent man, a charming talker, who makes it a point to use his wit to make the trip seem shorter to his passengers.

M. Betsellère, the steward, has already had the *good luck* of being shipwrecked. He was on board the *Gironde*, when that vessel came into collision with the *Louisiane* and foundered.

He had a miraculous escape; and now he is not afraid of anything. *Il en a vu bien d'autres !*

Our very youthful surgeon, M. Flamant, is also crossing the Atlantic for the first time. Poor doctor! His medicine was of no avail against sea-sickness.

We had not been gone two days before he ceased to appear at the table, and I took a cunning pleasure in sending every morning to inquire how he was getting on.

Among the passengers was, first of all, Mademoiselle Aimée, who had just returned from a very successful season in Russia; Boulard, whom I was taking with me as orchestra leader, and who had his young wife with him; M. Bacquero, a charming American, firmly resolved to introduce me to his compatriots, and who had succeeded, with the aid of the mighty dollar, in persuading me to undertake this little artistic tour; Arigotti, a *tenore robusto*, pupil of the Paris Conservatory, who, having lost his voice, had found a situation as secretary to M. Bacquero. He was a good pianist, and hail-fellow well met, with everybody on board; two pretty Philadelphia ladies; a few tradesmen going on to see the Exhibition, and a few exhibitors going on to trade; finally, a few travellers of no consequence. I cannot give a better idea of our trip than by quoting here the few lines I sent to my wife after landing:

"The first two days passed off very well. The weather was superb. I slept admirably on the Saturday while we touched at Plymouth. I had become quite accustomed to the rocking motion of the ship—so well accustomed that, when on Sunday night she suddenly stopped, I started up out of my sleep. My limited experience of sea voyages induced me to suppose that this sudden stoppage was the result of an accident. I jumped out of my berth, dressed in double quick time, and went on deck.

"It was a false alarm. The ship was under way again; but my sleep had left me, and with it a good deal of my confidence. I lay down without undressing, fearing that an accident might happen at any moment; for every few minutes the ship stopped, her screw being out of order.

"As if this were not enough, a storm came on to complicate the situation. For three days and four nights we were horribly tossed and tumbled about. The rolling and pitching were frightful. Inside the ship everything that was not made particularly fast was soon knocked to pieces; it was equally difficult to stand up or sit down. On the Monday my cabin became so uncomfortable, that I had to ask leave to sleep in the saloon. The captain and the whole ship's company were most kind and considerate to me. They remained with me part of the night, and endeavored by every possible means to persuade me there was no danger.

"'It is splendid,' the captain said to me; 'just come up and see how the ship dashes right into the waves, only to come out magnificently a minute afterwards!'

"'My dear captain,' I answered, 'to see a

tempest at a distance must be frightfully interesting; but I must say, that to play a part in the piece, as one of the actors, has, to my mind, but precious little fun in it.'

"Let me give you a characteristic trait of a young American girl, who was on board with her sister. At the very worst of the storm, when more than one was quietly saying his prayers and commending his soul to God (I wasn't the last to do so, I assure you!), the little American girl said to her sister: 'Sister, you really ought to try to get down and fetch my pretty little hat. I would like to die with all my fine things on.' 'Shall we bring up your gloves too?' quietly rejoined the younger one.

"Before entering the harbor, the *Canada* stopped at the two little islands known as the Quarantine, where the health and custom-house officers pay their usual visits to the ship.

"When a ship has any sick persons on board, they are landed on the first of these islands; and when they get better, they are taken to the other, where they remain until quite well.

"Formerly these two islands did not exist. It was on the Long Island shore that the vessels stopped to wait for the custom-house officers and the doctors. The inhabitants of this locality where wholly indifferent to the custom-house officers; but not so to the doctors, who bothered them immensely with their sick. The Long Islanders objected strongly to the unceasing importation of plague-stricken people who were sent to them from the four points of the globe. They finally declared one day that, in future, Long Island should not serve as a hospital, and that, even if they had to fire on the vessels, they would no longer allow them to land their sick on the island. 'But where would you have us put them?' asked the Governor of the State of New York.

"'Put them on the island opposite; we have had them long enough! It is Staten Island's turn now!'

"The Governor thought this demand, supported by rifles and shot-guns, sufficiently well founded to justify him in giving the order to transport the quarantine to the above-named island.

"The inhabitants of Staten Island, however, did not content themselves with threats; they went into open rebellion, and quietly set fire to the first ships which attempted to land, without inquiring whether or not they carried plague-stricken passengers.

"The authorities were not a little puzzled. But in America it is not the custom to remain long puzzled. The board met, and resolved that, since the two inhabited islands would not consent, under any circumstances, to receive the sick, two other islands should be constructed on which there should be no inhabitants. A short time afterwards the two islands now before us rose out of the sea as if by magic. The whole spirit of the American people is revealed by this feat.

"As we were expected the evening before, they had organized an excursion to meet me.

"Vessels, decorated with flags and Venetian lanterns, had on board newspaper men, sight-seers, a military band of sixty to eighty pieces, and waited for me at Sandy Hook; but, as we did not come, the vessel put farther out to sea, still hoping to meet us. They were jolly on board;

they sang, they laughed, the band played *our* prettiest tunes; but, as they got out, sea-sickness began to assert its rights, and the musicians were not the last to feel its effects, which produced the same result as that in Haydn's comic symphony, where the musicians disappear one after the other, putting out the lights as they go—only that ours had no lights to put out; but, instead of giving forth sounds, they gave forth, one after another, their souls to the sea.

"We were soon hailed by another craft, having on board the chief reporters of the New York press. You will understand that I took all the pains in the world not to make quite a fool of myself; and I assure you that upon our arrival at New York, two hours afterwards, we were already very good friends.

"At night, on returning from the theatre (for on the very first day I went to two theatres), I saw a crowd assembled in front of my hotel; electric lights everywhere, so that you would have imagined yourself in broad daylight. Above the balcony of the hotel was an inscription in big letters: 'Welcome, Offenbach.' An orchestra of some sixty musicians were serenading me. They played *Orphée*, the *Grande Duchesse*, etc. I dare not tell you of all the cheering, the shouts of 'Hurrah for Offenbach!' I was forced to appear on the balcony, just like Gambetta, and I shouted out a tremendous 'Thank you, gentlemen!' a polite utterance which, I trust, will not be suspected of subversive intentions.

"On Saturday I was invited to a dinner, given in my honor by the Lotos Club, one of the first clubs here — literary men, artists, merchants, bankers, many newspaper men of all shades of opinion. I send you the *menu* of the dinner.

"'I knew,' I said, in reply to a toast, 'that for a long time I had been liked by the Americans as a composer, and I hoped that when I had the honor of being better known to them I should also be liked as a man. I propose,' I added, 'a toast to the United States, but not the United States purely and simply. Inasmuch as the arts, like nations, are kindred, I propose the States—United to Europe!' *

* Les Etats—Unis à l'Europe.

"This speech, which the excitement of the moment can alone excuse, was loudly cheered. Yesterday (Monday) I was invited to the Press Club. Nothing but newspaper men, charming fellows, witty all, the majority speaking French very well, many of them having spent more or less time in France. Plenty of speeches addressed to me, and to which I replied as best I could."

# CHAPTER III.

### NEW YORK—GILMORE'S GARDEN.

On arriving at New York, I put up at the Fifth Avenue Hotel, which deserves a description, as in Europe one can form no idea of this kind of establishment. There is every convenience at hand; a dressing-room, bath, and closet are provided for each room. The ground floor of the hotel is an immense bazar—a little commercial city, in which every trade is represented. There is the hair-dresser of the hotel, the hatter, the tailor, the druggist, the bookseller, even the boot-black of the hotel. One might arrive at a hotel as lightly dressed as Adam before the fall, as long-haired as Absalom before he caught in the tree, and depart as respectable as the famous Comte d'Orsay of fashionable memory. Everything is to be found in the Fifth Avenue Hotel —everything. with the exception, however, of a polyglot; this alone is entirely wanting. Among the two hundred waiters of this gigantic establishment you would seek in vain for one who spoke French. This is not very pleasant for those who cannot speak English; but, in compensation for this, what numberless comforts!

For twenty dollars a day you have a bed-room and sitting-room, with all the conveniences just enumerated, and the right of eating all day long. From eight to eleven o'clock, there is breakfast; from twelve to three in the afternoon, lunch; from five to seven, dinner; from eight to eleven, tea. The dining-room is on the first floor; as soon as you appear at the door of this immense hall, where fifty tables are methodically arranged, the steward meets you, and shows you to a seat. Resistance, fancy or preference for one corner rather than for another, are vain. The *maître d'hôtel* (steward) is also master of the hotel, and will place next to you whoever he chooses, without as much as asking your leave. When you are seated, the waiter, without asking what you will take, brings you a large glass of ice-water; for there is one thing worthy of note in America: it is, that, of all the fifty tables in the room, there is not one upon which anything but ice-water is drunk; if by chance you see wine or beer before a guest, you may be certain that he is a European.

After the glass of water, the waiter hands you the list of the eighty dishes of the day—I do not exaggerate; you make your choice, selecting three or four; and the most comical part of the business is, that all you have ordered is brought you at once. If you have unfortunately forgotten to mention the vegetables you desire, then the fifteen vegetables down on the bill-of-fare will all be brought you at the same time. So that you find yourself suddenly surrounded by thirty dishes—soup, fish, meat, vegetables, and sweets, without counting the rear-guard of desserts, which is always composed of at least a dozen varieties. All is arranged before you, bidding defiance to your stomach; the first time it makes you dizzy and takes away all appetite.

I will say no more about American hotels for the moment, as I intend to give a more minute description of them hereafter. I breakfast hurriedly, for my one wish, my one desire since arriving, is to see the famous covered Garden where, as Bilboquet would say, I am about to display my talents; I hastened then to Gilmore's Garden.

Imagine a vast covered garden. In the centre of a great mass of tropical plants stands the stage, large enough to accommodate an orchestra of a hundred to a hundred and twenty musicians. All around are grass-plots, shrubbery, and flower-beds, among which the public circulate. Facing the entry is a large cascade, which imitates Niagara Falls during the interludes. The corners of the Garden are occupied by little Swiss cottages, which can hold seven or eight persons, and which advantageously supply the place of boxes in a theatre. A large gallery, with ordinary boxes and tiers of seats, afford facilities for those who like seeing and hearing from an elevation, to satisfy their taste.

The *ensemble* reminds one somewhat of the old *Jardin d'Hiver*, once so popular in the Champs-Elysées. The hall has a capacity of eight to nine thousand persons. It is brilliantly lit up; colored glasses are hung in festoons of the most picturesque effect.

Delighted with the hall, I asked Mr. Grau, the manager, a few particulars upon the orchestra I was to lead.

"We have engaged," he answered me, "the hundred and ten musicians you asked for; and I can assure you they are the best in New York."

I soon discovered that he had not deceived me.

I had the rare good fortune of gaining the sympathy of my orchestra from the start; and here is how it happened: The musicians have here a vast and powerful organization, and have constituted a society, outside of which there is no salvation. Any one who wishes to join an orchestra must first become a member of the society. There is no exception to this rule; from the leader to the drummer inclusively, all must belong to it.

I had been advised of this state of things by Boulard, who had already led one or two rehearsals, and who had been obliged to join the association in order to be allowed to lead.

On my entering the hall, the musicians received me with a regular ovation, for which I returned thanks in a few words.

We begin the rehearsal with the overture of "*Vert-Vert.*" I had scarcely led sixteen bars when I stopped the orchestra, and, addressing the musicians:

"Excuse me, gentlemen," I said. "We have scarcely begun, and you have already failed in your duty."

General astonishment.

"What! I am not a member of your association, and you allow me to lead!"

Whereupon there was a general laugh. I waited until this had subsided, and then added, quite seriously:

"Since you have not thought proper to mention it to me, I must myself request to be admitted into your society."

They protested; but I insisted, saying that I entirely approved of their institution, and should consider it an honor to belong to it.

My request was received with long and loud applause. I had conquered my orchestra, and from this moment we were all members of the same family, and the most perfect *harmony* never ceased to prevail among us. It is fair to add that the orchestra was composed in a superior manner; for each of my pieces two rehearsals were always sufficient to insure a most brilliant rendering.

## CHAPTER IV.

THE HOUSES—THE STREETS—THE CARS.

I DID not stay long in the Fifth Avenue Hotel, where they eat so much, and where they speak so little French. After three or four days I went to reside at a private house in Madison Square. Here again I was able to judge to what extent comfort is carried in America. Not only are there furnaces supplying heat for all the apartments, gas in all the rooms, hot and cold water at all times, but on the ground floor there are three pretty little knobs, of great importance. These three knobs represent three considerable forces: protection of the law, help in case of accident, and the services of an assistant. All this represented by three knobs? Certainly; and there is no magic about it either!

The three knobs are electric ones; you press upon the first, and a porter appears to take your orders. You touch the second, and a policeman comes to place himself at your disposition. The third knob enables you to give the alarm, in case of fire, and brings, in a few seconds, a whole brigade of firemen around your house.

Nor is this all. Besides these three knobs you may, if you choose, have in your study what is to be found in all the leading hotels, bar-rooms, eating-houses, public-houses, and even cigar-stores, viz.: the telegraph. You have only to express the desire, and they will set up in your house a little apparatus which will function from morning till night and from night till morning, and which gives you all the news from both worlds. A continuous slip of paper, unrolling in a wicker basket, enables you to read the last dispatches from Paris, the news of the war in the East, as well as of the elections in Cincinnati or St. Louis. At all hours you can ascertain the rise or fall of all the stock markets in the world, and can see whether you have made or lost a fortune.

If the New York houses are extremely practical, the city itself is organized in a marvellous manner. The Americans do not, like us, name their streets after the people who govern, nor change the names of the streets every time a government disappears; it would not do for that republic which changes its President every four years. At the end of twenty years a street would have had more names than the most renowned hidalgos of Castille. To avoid the inconvenience of this system, the Americans prefer naming their streets and their avenues by numbers:. First Avenue, Second Avenue; this has nothing to do with politics, and needs no change. In the squares, which are magnificent, but few statues are to be seen; there is one of Washington, a very modest one. This is a great contrast to France, where everybody is more or less sculptured in marble or moulded in bronze, in consequence of which our country begins to look like an immense museum of men in frock-coats, or a collection of dummies for a ready-made clothing-store.

From my window I discovered in Madison Square a curious and charming feature. On the upper branches of the trees are placed little houses, half hid in the foliage. These are to lodge the sparrows brought from Europe; these little birds, brought from their mother country, are the objects of the greatest attention; the law protects them, and it is forbidden to touch them; they are as much respected as the pigeons of Saint Mark.

Most of the streets are literally spoilt by the rails which cross them in every direction; these are used for the tramways, to which here they give the name of *cars*.

The American car is not at all like our French vehicles, not even like those which Parisians call American omnibuses. The number of passengers is not limited; although all the seats may be occupied, there is always room; the last comers stand holding on to straps which hang from the inside, or crowd upon the platform; in case of necessity, they would sit on the conductor's shoulders; so long as there is a projection free, a knee vacant, a step unoccupied, the car is not considered full. A car, which is built for twenty-four persons, thus often carries three times as many from one end of the town to another, and for the modest sum of five cents.

Americans, who are shrewd fellows, have found the way to utilize for their private account the numerous rails which are laid on nearly every street, by making the wheels of their carriages to fit the tracks; in this manner they go faster, and fatigue their horses less; they leave the tracks merely to pass ahead of the heavy cars of the company.

Sometimes the cars come at full speed behind them, before they have time to get out of the way; but an accident of this kind is soon repaired: the horses scramble to their feet, the driver climbs upon his box without grumbling, and quietly returns to the track as soon as the car has gone by. The omnibuses, which do not go on rails, have no conductor to receive the money; the passenger himself pays his fare, by dropping the change in a little box placed for the purpose.

I asked an American, if the company did not lose much money by this system; he replied that it would cost dearer to pay a conductor, and some one to look after him, and that they lost less in trusting to the honesty of the passengers. The practical side of the Americans is seen in the most trifling details; the little box, of which I have just spoken, answers two purposes: during the day it receives the pennies; in the evening it is lit up and becomes a lantern. A great number of vehicles are covered by gigantic parasols, which serve to protect the coachmen from the heat, which is terrible, and to bear advertisements. I was told that this monster parasol was changed every week at the expense of the advertiser. The success of the cars, which pass every minute or two, is considerable, as this kind of locomotion has quite entered into American habits; even the ladies and the richest people make use of it; and they are right, for cabs or coaches, with one or two horses, are excessively dear. It is true they are comfortable and well kept; but it is hard to pay a dollar and a half, for a ride in a one-horse cab; those with two horses cost two dollars—seven francs and a half, and ten francs; and should you omit to settle on a price in advance, they would ask you, for a drive to the Central Park, seven dollars—thirty-five francs for a two hours' drive.

While the great number of cars and omnibuses which circulate through the streets of New York offer evident advantages, they also present serious dangers for foot-passengers; therefore, at most of the busiest crossings, passage-ways laid in flag-stones have been established, and a policeman has charge, to see that pedestrians are not run over; he fulfils his duty in the most paternal manner, taking ladies and children by the hand, leading them to the opposite side of the street, stopping all the carriages on the crossing. This precaution is much appreciated by the American ladies, who readily go out of their way to be piloted across by the agent of the public force. I was told that, should one be run over on the crossing, a large amount of damages could be recovered by the injured party; but if this misfortune should occur at a time when you happen to be on the pavement, just outside the crossing, not only you have no right to recover anything, but the owner of the carriage can demand damages for his loss of time.

# CHAPTER V.

### THE THEATRES OF NEW YORK.

One of my first cares, on arriving at New York, was to visit such theatres as were still open.

The principal theatres of the city are admirably well managed; they are all built on the same plan, in the form of a vast amphitheatre, with several tiers of seats, in long rows; there are generally only eight boxes in each of them—four proscenium boxes on the right, and four on the left. Even these few boxes are almost always empty, even when the rest of the building is crowded. The best society prefers seats in the orchestra or dress circle.

As there are very few managers who are permanently in the business, the theatres are let for a season, a month, or even a week.

A manager has the right to fail two or three

times; he is not thought the worse of for such a trifling thing as that; the deeper he plunges, the quicker he returns to the surface.

They showed me a highly respected manager, who had managed to fail six or seven times.

"He is very clever," they told me; "next winter he will bring out a splendid company."

I asked how he would find the money.

"The persons to whom he owes," they replied, "keep lending him in hopes that he will succeed some day, and that they will have a chance to recover what they have lost."

They perform grand operas at the Academy of Music; but I was unable to see one, as during eight months the theatre had only been open some sixty times.

There had been four weeks of fair success, when Tietiens appeared in *Norma*; then, Strakosch arrived with Bellocca, who did not have much success, notwithstanding the tremendous puffing which had preceded her.

The most brilliant periods of this theatre were during the engagements of Nilsson, of Lucca, of Morel, of Capoul, and of Campanini. At Booth's

Theatre, tragedy, comedy, or opera are played, according to the fancy of the manager who hires the theatre. I saw *Henry the Fifth* played there by an actor of merit, Mr. Rignold; the scenery was very fine.

One week later the *North Star* was played on the same stage, with Miss Kellogg, an American singer, between thirty-two or thirty-four years of age, and who has a very fine voice. Meyerbeer's opera, not having been sufficiently rehearsed, totally lacked *ensemble*, especially in the finale of the second act. The chorus and the orchestra seemed engaged in an unsuccessful game of hide and seek. Upon the whole, it was not unlike the performance of one of Wagner's weakest works.

A rather funny thing, however, was to see, among the spectators in the orchestra stalls, a number of trombones and bassoons, who put in a note from time to time. I must say this puzzled me. Who were these musicians? Were they amateurs, trombones by vocation, who had come voluntarily to strengthen the orchestra? I had not to wait long for an explanation: a glance was sufficient to discover the cause of this anomaly. The space allotted to the orchestra was not large enough, and the brass instruments had been removed outside the railing.

At the Union Square Theatre I heard *Ferréol* in English, with a first-class company. I attended, also, a performance of *Conscience*—a very good play, by two young American authors, Messrs. Lancaster and Magnus. In the same house, I was told, *Rose Michel* had been performed with immense success.

On the evening of my visit to Wallack's Theatre the four hundredth performance of the *Mighty Dollar* was given, and the principal parts were played by Mr. and Mrs. Florence, both actors of superior ability. They reminded me, the first of our excellent Geoffroy, the latter of our lively Alphonsine. This pair of artists have been playing together for more than twenty years, and enjoy great favor with the Americans. The perfect concert of the other actors, in their performance, was quite remarkable. I noticed particularly a charming *ingénue*, scarcely seventeen years of age, Miss Baker, who does honor to her part as a youthful prima-donna; and I must not forget to mention the elegant and sympathetic Miss Cummins.

Mr. Deutsch, manager of Wallack's, is one of the youngest as also one of the cleverest New York managers. Some idea may be formed of American theatrical management by the re-engagement of Mr. and Mrs. Florence for four hundred nights. Mr. Deutsch expects to visit with them all the principal cities of the Union, from New York to San Francisco—giving always the same play, the *Mighty Dollar.*

The Lyceum Theatre was closed for the summer season. In this theatre Fechter had great success, in the *Dame aux Camélias* and in several other plays. Dramas with chorus and orchestra have also been frequently performed here.

In the Lyceum Theatre the first attempt was made to remove the orchestra out of sight of the public, a novelty lately renewed by Wagner at Bayreuth. The nuisance of this innovation was soon found out. First of all, the acoustics were wretched. Then the musicians, who were crowded into a subterranean receptacle, suffering from the excessive heat, undertook to remedy the difficulty as best they could.

On the first evening a fiddler removed his cravat, and unbuttoned his waistcoat; on the following night the altos took off their coats, and played in their shirt-sleeves; and within a week all the musicians were doing as much. Finally, one evening the public perceived, rising from beneath the stage, a light cloud of smoke; there was at once a real panic: it proved to be only the musicians enjoying a smoke. This was the last of this foolish innovation. The musicians put on their coats, and returned to their accustomed position.

Another theatre, which I was unable to see, is the Grand Opera House, which was likewise closed. This was built by the famous Fisk, who was assassinated by his friend Stokes. This Fisk was one of the most eccentric and famous New York characters: the son of poor parents, he earned his livelihood, when a youth, by selling small wares and hair-oil. He became not only manager of the largest theatre in New York, but also vice-president of a railway company, commodore of a line of steamers, and colonel of a regiment.

He was bold and energetic in his enterprises, and showed great originality in his ways. Every person who wanted employment on his railway had first to enlist in his regiment; and in this manner he organized one of the finest regiments in New York. Occasionally he would take a fancy to call out his men, and have them march gallantly in presence of some fair dame. On such occasions the railway traffic was suspended, and the stations were closed along the whole line.

This magnificent colonel possessed splendid carriages and horses, and never drove out otherwise than in a beautiful open carriage, drawn by eight fine horses.

His tragic death was the result of a love affair; the great impresario fell a victim to a domestic tragedy, and a two-fold vengeance stopped his career. Here are the facts:

Fisk fell hopelessly in love with a beautiful American lady, to whom he became desperately attached. Wondrous theatrical performances were given in her honor; parades of the famous regiment, with the consequent stoppage of his railway—he set everything to work to carry his point, and of course he succeeded. In accordance with the immutable law of nature, the first thing Fisk did was to introduce his friend Stokes to his mistress. Since the days of King Candaulus, lovers have always been equally foolish. Stokes had a goodly income; he was charmed with the lady; and Fisk became .... the happiest of the three, until the day when he discovered the treachery of his friend.

I cannot say whether his first impulse was or not to seize his revolver; but I do know that, on second thought, he gave up this solution as insufficient; he had imagined a better plan. Without manifesting in any way to his friend Stokes the hatred he had conceived towards him, he pretended, on the contrary, to have become more attached to him than ever. He persuaded him to take part with him in different speculations, and to invest all his money in certain stocks which he was "bulling" at the time; then he threw all his own shares upon the market, overstocked the market, and brought about a terrible fall, which completed the ruin of his good friend Stokes. I presume that Fisk was so pleased with the result of his little combination, that he had a little conversation with Stokes, and explained to him the why and wherefore of his ruin. Stokes, who probably could not see the joke, swore on his side to revenge himself. But as he had not the cunning of his enemy, he had recourse to a more vulgar and more expeditious means. He waited one day for Fisk until he came out of the Grand Central Hotel, where the aforesaid beautiful lady resided, and quietly blew out his brains.

If Fisk had survived, no doubt he would have had a fine drama written on this subject for his theatre.

The last theatre which I visited was the Fifth Avenue Theatre, a very handsome one, where a heavy drama, *Pique,* was being performed. The play was made up of situations stolen almost everywhere, but is, of course, by Mr. Boucicault.

There are also two German and one French theatre in New York; they are open from time to time, whenever they happen to find a manager.

But I must not close this chapter on American theatres without mentioning a little hall where I heard the minstrels.

There all the actors are negroes; the chorus consists of negroes; the servants are negroes; —cashier, manager, superintendent, men and women, all black!

On sighting the stage, I perceived a negro orchestra, playing tunes more or less fantastic.

But great was my surprise on becoming aware that I was the object of their special attention, and that they were pointing me out to one another. I could not believe that I was known to so many negroes; but, nevertheless, I must confess I was delighted to find that such was the case.

The performance was sufficiently comical to induce me to remain to the end. What was my astonishment on returning, after the first act, to witness a renewal of the same manifestations towards me—that is to say, the musicians again pointing me out to one another. This time they were all white, as white as the bakers in the Boulangère. I became prouder than ever; but, alas! there was deception in store for me. I was informed they were the same musicians, and that, from the manager to the servants, they were nothing but sham negroes, who alternately painted and washed their faces three or four times every evening, according to the requirements of the performances.

# CHAPTER VI.

ART IN AMERICA.

The foreigner's attention is attracted by thousands of admirable objects on his visit to the United States. In America, more than anywhere else, human intelligence and labor have worked miracles. It would be superfluous to praise the manufacturing industry, so thoroughly organized, so powerfully assisted by machinery, the strength and power of which astound the imagination. It would be idle to call up the marvels accomplished upon this land, virgin still scarce a hundred years ago; nor to speak of the vast network of railways and telegraphs spreading its links farther and farther every day; and of the numerous other improvements which constantly tend to increase the comforts of life.

But a sad thought occurs to disturb the traveller's admiration, when he observes that the distribution of forces is not equally balanced in their employment, and that the progress, which made the United States so great, was only directed to one side: they have conquered the material world, but have remained behind in the acquisition of those qualities essential to spiritual life. America is to-day like a giant of a hundred cubits, endowed with every physical gift, but lacking the one essential thing—a soul.

Art is the soul of nations; it expresses in words what the purest sentiments create.

My chapter on the theatres will already have suggested the thought that the dramatic art was sadly neglected in the United States, and has served to show its present deplorable condition.

Good actors, well trained companies, and authors are only produced by stable institutions, steady local work, and slowly acquired traditions. But there is no permanent opera in New York, no comic opera, nor even a theatre for operettes which is sure to last for two consecutive years; and there is no stage for classic or modern plays which could offer sufficient guarantees of stability to become a school; for in America the stage lives from hand to mouth. Manager and company are nomadic, and the greater number of actors are mere travellers borrowed from the Old World, who arrive and depart with the season.

The same observation applies also to other branches of art, and neither music, painting, nor sculpture find in America a soil which favors their development. You may assert that there are painters and sculptors; I agree with you, and I know myself several of eminent talent: Bierstadt, Hunt, Ball, Church, Vinnie Ream, and many others. Where is the moor on which no flower grows? I see a few flowers, but I see no garden; and if there are good painters, still there is no American school.

It is all-important for the glory of the United States to remedy this great deficiency. A nation of such magnitude must not lack one essential quality which art alone could add to the splendor and glory of their industrial power.

What are the best means of developing the fine arts in the United States? Were I called upon to answer this question, I would say to the Americans:

4*

You possess all the necessary elements—intelligent and talented men; and, as a proof that you lack no capacity, I again refer to the artists' names already mentioned, who have succeeded, without means of culture, and under unfavorable circumstances, in producing masterpieces. You have wealth and excellent amateur collections, which are justly celebrated. Employ these elements, and you will command success.

If your principles forbid the State to aid this reform by subsidies, then you must organize yourselves. European States support only a few leading theatres in their capitals, and the theatres and museums in the smaller towns are aided by the municipal authority. In our country the city councils do much for the progress of art; they provide not alone for theatres and museums, but often give free admissions to conservatories and academies, to young persons who show a natural disposition for the fine arts. You can easily imitate this example; if the municipality cannot help you, you can establish great societies and corresponding associations in all the principal cities, for the protection of art.

As the material means abound with you, you can with their assistance accomplish the same that government institutions do in Europe.

Your subsidies can help to establish theatres and elevate dramatic art, procure permanent managers, protected to a degree against bankruptcy. Two operas and one literary stage are needed: above all, a national conservatory, where you can form talented scholars; but you must provide for them eminent teachers and professors of distinction from Europe, and retain them with you. When you have once permanent theatres and a well-appointed conservatory, you will have aided greatly the dramatic art and American composers and authors. However, you will not reap the fruits immediately. There might elapse perhaps ten, twenty years, before these institutions produce the excellent results that may be expected of them. And what are twenty years? In twenty years your students may become masters; you will be independent of European art; and ten years later the theatres of the Old World may require your actors, as you now require theirs.

And are the other branches of art not required in the same way? You must establish museums. Often have men discovered in themselves the creative qualities which God bestowed upon them, or those faculties of assimilation which frequently are equivalent to genius; good taste is formed and purified by the contemplation of masterpieces.

You want likewise academies for painting and sculpture, with professors chosen from our best institutes. The masters will not consent to leave their country; but the greatest painters and the greatest sculptors are not what you need, as those next them have all necessary qualities for teaching; and these you must invite. Don't consider the cost, for then only can you found an American school worthy to appear in the records of art, by the side of the Italians, Dutch, Spaniards, and Frenchmen. A hundred years have sufficed to raise the United States to the highest point of industrial splendor, and a nation which has given such admirable proofs of energy, activity, and perseverance, requires but a short time to acquire a rank in the dominions of art.

# CHAPTER VII.

RESTAURANTS—THREE TYPES OF WAITERS.

There are many restaurants in New York and Philadelphia.

At the Brunswick, which is French, the table is very good; at Delmonico's, which is Swiss, it is not quite so good; and at the Hoffman, which is German, it is only tolerable. Other New York restaurants are Morelli (Italian) and Frascati (Spanish), where you can dine for one dollar. I saw many other restaurants, enormously frequented, but I could not vouch for their fare. The Brunswick has an advantage over Delmonico's: an immense hall, such as could not be found in Paris.

Pétry (French) and Finelli (Italian) are the most popular establishments in Philadelphia, if I leave out Verdier, who is there only for the time, and whose dining-saloons are at the Exhibition, two hours' distance from the city.

As you see, there are in fact no restaurants which can properly be called American.

The Americans keep the hotels, but the kitchen seems entirely surrendered to foreigners. Nothing is easier than to eat a meal in the French, Italian, Spanish, or German style. Nothing is more difficult for a stranger than to eat an American dinner in America.

I had almost forgotten to mention the most interesting of all restaurants—the restaurant that *serves meals gratis!*

It would certainly never occur to one of our French hotel-keepers to open a free *table d'hôte*. In spite of the Irishman's assertion, that it is possible to get rich while losing on each article by making it up on the quantity, neither Bignon, nor Brébant, nor the Café Riche have yet made such an attempt; and one must really go to a progressive country in order to see such things.

At all events, several well-known New York restaurants serve meals for nothing—provided you take a drink, even if it only cost ten cents. On Sundays, when, thanks to the police, the restaurants dare not sell drinks, it is all the better for the consumer. Lunch is served as usual, and I can state this as a fact, having seen it at the Brunswick myself; and they say that living is expensive in America.

And it must not be supposed that this gratuitous meal is composed of mere trifles. Here is a bill of fare, copied on the spot:

Ham.

An enormous piece of roast-beef.

Pork and beans.

Potato salad.

Olives, pickles, etc.

Cheese.

Crackers.

Wholesome and abundant fare as may be seen. The most substantial part is the roast-beef, from which the guests are privileged to cut, themselves, such slices as they like.

A large pile of plates stands on a sideboard, convenient free lunch, together with forks and knives, in abundance; but the guests, as a rule, prefer using their own fingers; some going so far as to help themselves by the handful out of the salad-bowl. I shudder still, just to think of it!

The head-waiter, to whom I expressed my horror and astonishment, tried his best to soothe my feelings.

"This offends us less than it does you. *Time is money*, you see; and these gentlemen are in such a hurry!"

Waiters in hotels and restaurants are often very peculiar types!

For instance, as I have already mentioned elsewhere, when you sit down at the table, a waiter brings you a glass of ice-water; you might sit there for two hours in company with your ice-water without anybody interfering with you.

You must call another waiter, who hands you the bill-of-fare. Meantime you are dying of thirst, and you want something else to drink besides water. The waiter who took your order goes leisurely for a third one, who brings you at last the desired drink; but you are mistaken if you think yourself safe now: it is another waiter who alone has the privilege of using the corkscrew. At least such is the case at the Brunswick. This annoying proceeding having occurred several times, I declared at last that I would leave the house if this farce was not dropped. When I came to breakfast the following morning, every one of the twenty or thirty waiters of the restaurant were drawn up in line on my passage, and every one gravely held a corkscrew in his hand. Since then the service at the Brunswick is considerably more prompt.

On the evening of my arrival in New York, I dined with some friends in my room at the Fifth Avenue Hotel. The soup had just been served, when I fancied I heard a sound like whistling. I looked around in astonishment to discover the bold individual. Of course, it was not one of the guests; it was the waiter. My first impulse was to get up and kick him out; but my friends, who had noticed the same extraordinary phenomenon, beckoned me to keep still. We continued our dinner. As to the musician, though timid at first, he became gradually bolder, and soon ventured upon little trills, finally essaying the most difficult pieces. At one time, as if overcome by sudden melancholy, he would indulge in the gloomiest of tunes; then suddenly, and without any apparent reason, the liveliest and merriest melodies burst forth from his lips.

The dinner over, I called the waiter's attention to the impropriety of which he had been guilty, in giving us music at the table without having been requested to do so.

"You see, sir, I love music, and I use it to express my thoughts. If a dish is not to my taste, I whistle melancholy airs; when a dish suits me, I whistle lively tunes. But when I fairly worship a dish . . . . "

"Like the frozen charlotte we had just now?" I interrupted.

"Monsieur noticed it? Oh! then I whistle my merriest tunes."

"And do you think that tune from the *Grande Duchesse* you were whistling just now particularly gay?"

"Your music, sir, is always so funny!"

I don't very much fancy hearing my music whistled; so I requested the steward in future not to send me a whistling waiter.

### Second Sketch of a Waiter.

This is rather curious too.

It was in Philadelphia I had the pleasure of meeting the fellow. It was half-past nine in the evening when we arrived in that city, and we were, my friends and myself, literally starved. Having inquired for a good restaurant, we were directed to Pétry's; so to Pétry's we went, and here we are at the table.

"Waiter!"

"Well, sir?"

"Give us first a good Julienne soup."

The waiter makes a wry face.

"I should not recommend it to you, sir; the vegetables here are so very tough."

"Well, never mind the soup; have you any salmon?"

"Oh! yes, sir, we have salmon, of course, and we have had it a good long time too; possibly it may not be as fresh as you might wish."

"How then about a Chateaubriand, nice and rare?"

"The cook don't know how to get them up, sir."

"Strawberries?"

"They are not fit to eat, sir."

"And the cheese?"

"I'll ask it to come up, sir; it is quite able to walk by itself."

"I say, waiter, you will never make your master's fortune."

"My first duty, sir, is to please my customers."

"If I was Mr. Pétry I would soon discharge you."

"Mr. Pétry did not wait for your advice, sir. You see me here to-night for the last time."

Whereupon he bowed to us in his best style; after which we had an excellent supper.

### *Waiter Number Three.*

Delmonico's waiters' style deserves a special mention.

We were invited one evening, by a theatrical manager, to a supper, in company with the leading actors of his theatre. The supper was excellent. Like all other good things, it came to an end. The time for a smoke and a chat having come, we remained in our parlor, smoking and sipping iced drinks. There was then no further necessity for the presence of a servant; nevertheless I noticed, not without astonishment, our waiter returning very often, and listening to our conversation. As I was not the host, I thought it best to say nothing. As to the other guests, none seemed to have noticed this strange proceeding.

When about to part, I took occasion to invite the manager and his artists to a supper in the same restaurant.

Supper over, the same occurrence took place. This time I observed the waiter more attentively, and I noticed that he went all around the table, examining closely every one of the guests. He went away after that, but returned within a few minutes and renewed his examination and his perambulations.

"Waiter, you have come several times without being called; let this be the last, please."

"Sorry, sir," he answered; "but we have orders from Mr. Delmonico to walk every five minutes into every parlor and private room."

"Is Mr. Delmonico connected with the police, then, that he sends you to listen to what his guests say?"

"Don't know, sir. Sure Mr. Delmonico would dismiss me if his instructions were not strictly obeyed."

"Is Mr. Delmonico afraid we are going to carry off his napkins and spoons; does he think we are likely to forget for a moment that a decent behavior is *de rigueur* in his famous restaurant? I am sorry to tell you, my friend; it is now half-past one, and we intend remaining here till seven; you will, therefore, have to repeat your visit sixty-six times more if you follow your instructions."

"I'll do it, sir."

I need not say that, after thus giving vent to our indignation, we did not carry out our threat. We left a little late (it was nearly two o'clock), vowing never to be caught again in this way.

New Yorkers, who don't care to have the whole town know in the morning how they spent the previous evening, will do well to keep an eye on those waiters who obey Mr. Delmonico's orders so punctually.

## CHAPTER VIII.

AMERICAN WOMEN—INTRODUCTIONS—CENTRAL PARK.

LADIES, and even young girls, enjoy here the greatest freedom. I have an idea that when Lafayette went to America to fight for Liberty, he only had the ladies in view, for they alone are really free in free America.

My friends Meilhac and Halévy, in the *Vie Parisienne*, assert that Parisian ladies alone possess the art of walking on the street; but they had not seen American women going, coming, getting out of the way of carriages, picking up their skirts with an elegant gesture, and revealing the most exquisite ankles with the most consummate skill.

It must be confessed that there are perhaps no women so fascinating as American women. In the first place, they are handsome in a proportion wholly unknown in Paris. Out of every hundred you meet, there are ninety who are lovely. Moreover, they know how to dress; their toilets are of the most exquisite and perfect taste. They look as if they had all just come from Worth's.

One thing alone I shall venture to criticise on their dress; that is, the little pocket, located just above the knee, where, in olden times, the ladies hung their purse. This pocket is exclusively devoted to the handkerchief. When, from a distance, a bit of white linen is seen issuing from this aperture, one is apt to wonder whether an accident has befallen the lady, and whether it is not a certain nameless garment which is thus revealed through a rent in the skirt.

All the American ladies you meet hold their purses tightly in their hands, lest some pickpocket—of which there are perhaps as many in New York as in Paris—should be tempted to thrust a profane hand in their pocket. *Shocking!* In the afternoon young girls may be seen alone visiting the first-class restaurants and taking their lunch as quietly as an old European bachelor. Others are seen on some corner of Fifth Avenue, or elsewhere, waiting for their carriages, to which they have given orders to meet them, and drive to Central Park.

A strange fact for the depraved Parisian who is fond of following pretty women on the street, is that no one in New York or in any other city of the United States would venture to take up his line of march behind a youthful Yankee maiden, and still less to speak to her, even to offer her an umbrella.

In order to be able to offer her this object, with or without your heart, you must be presented, or *introduced*, as they say. But do not imagine that the formalities of an introduction are either very formidable or very difficult to accomplish. In the absence of a common friend, a simple "Personal" in the *Herald* will answer.

I spoke of the Central Park just now. It is the favorite drive of the most elegant society; but it does not in any way resemble our Bois de Bologne. Imagine a great rocky plain, skillfully concealed beneath well-kept lawns, a few groves of fine trees, one or two little lakes, and magnificent drives; such is the New York

*Bois.* Every day a procession of carriages may be seen there more numerous than on an Italian *corso*. American carriage manufacturers seem particularly bent upon inventing the most fantastic vehicles, all of which belong in a degree, more or less remote, to two leading styles: the first, which is enormously heavy, is a kind of landau of the Middle Ages, a massive coach, a monster berline, which, it is true, is capable of accommodating many people quite comfortably. But the aspect of these houses on wheels remains always horrible. A large window behind, with an ever-dangling curtain, makes it higher still. The other style, on the contrary, is of extreme lightness. It consists of a diminutive box, with or without top, seating one or two persons at most, and mounted on four great wheels, so thin and so slender that they impart to the carriage the appearance of a huge spider. These buggies, as they are called, have sometimes their tops raised; but as this is open on all sides, they always look as if they were in rags. It is not rare to see young ladies of the highest classes driving alone one of these light vehicles drawn by two powerful horses.

The first time I visited Central Park it was in company with a gentleman well known in New York, and at almost every step he met some friend. I noticed that he bowed very low to some, while to others he scarcely touched the brim of his hat. I asked him what it meant. He replied, quite seriously: "The gentleman to whom I have just bowed so respectfully belongs to the best New York society, and is worth a million of dollars. The one coming now is only worth a hundred thousand, and so he does not stand as well as the former one; I treat him, therefore, with less ceremony."

These are shades which are observed in America, where there is no aristocracy save that of labor and of the dollar.

# CHAPTER IX.

### THE STORY OF TWO STATUES.

EVER generous France said to herself, one fine morning: "What can I do to be agreeable to America?" Then the idea occurred to her that it might be well to remind the New World that Lafayette had not been wholly a stranger in the establishment of its liberties.

At once a telegram was sent by the sub-marine cable to President Grant.

This dispatch was very brief, as every word costs seventy-five cents (gold). It read thus:

"Grant, President; Whitehouse, Washington: Wish to please you much. Want to build statue Lafayette for your beautiful country. What think you? Reply prepaid."

The answer came promptly.

Here is a copy of it, as communicated to me:

"Wish to please you much. See no objection

to proposition. Go on, build statue Lafayette; forward well packed, and free of charges. Grateful America."

This occurred when M. Thiers was President. An appropriation was at once voted, and one of our most skillful sculptors, M. Bartholdi, was commissioned to place himself at once in communication with Lafayette. Three months later the statue was finished, and delivered to the Minister.

For a whole year nothing more was heard of it.

Some Frenchmen, residing in the United States, becoming anxious on the subject, requested a merchant who was going to Europe on business to ascertain the whereabouts of the statue.

The merchant promptly called on M. Thiers, not being aware that M. Thiers was no longer in office.

"You must go to my successor," said M. Thiers.

The merchant then called on the President, who granted him an interview, and gave him this piece of advice: "Apply at the proper department."

Having discovered the proper department, the gentleman is kindly received, and is told: "Apply to the Director of the Fine Arts."

The Director is fortunately at home.

The merchant is thereupon shown to his private office, and the following conversation takes place:

"I wish to find out something about Lafayette's statue."

"Wait a minute. My chief clerk will probably be able to tell you; as to myself, I have only been here a few days."

The chief clerk is sent for.

"Do you know anything of a statue of Lafayette?"

"It is packed away in the cellar," he replies, gravely.

"Then, sir, will you please order it brought up, and shipped immediately, freight prepaid, to the United States?"

But I have no orders from the Minister, sir! Even if I had, I have no funds available for this shipment."

"The statue cannot forever remain in the cellar. France has promised it to America. America impatiently awaits it."

"I do not wish to hinder you from taking it away, sir; I'll say more: I fully authorize you to do so."

Our merchant was determined not to return without his Lafayette. Besides he had his own idea, and proceeded to carry it out. He found the statue, and had it shipped at once to New York, consigned to the French Consul-General.

Shortly after, having himself returned to New York, he promptly called on our Consul-General, when the following conversation took place:

"Well, Mr. Consul-General, I have just returned from France."

"Welcome, sir."

"I have brought it with me."

"Brought what?"

"The statue."

"What statue?"

"The statue of Lafayette."

"Glad to hear it," replies the Consul.

"I had it shipped in bond."

"All right, sir."

"And consigned to you."

"To me? What for, pray?"

"Because it's you who will have to pay the freight and duties."

"Freight? I? The Government has given me no orders to that effect."

"Come, now, Mr. Consul-General, it is only a trifling matter of a few thousand francs."

Of course, the Consul could not be persuaded. Fortunately for our traveller and his statue, a French committee had been formed in America, and had the funds ready for delivering the unfortunate Lafayette from the clutches of the custom-house. The most curious part of the story, however, is, that the redeemed Lafayette has made no further progress since, and, at the moment of this writing, no suitable place has yet been found whereon to erect it.

France, growing more and more generous, said to herself one fine morning: "What could I do to be agreeable to America on the occasion of her Centennial? Suppose I present her with a statue?"

All right for a statue, then. A subscription

was opened; Frenchmen and Americans both contributed, and it was unanimously resolved that the statue should represent *Liberty enlightening the World.* M. Bartholdi—above mentioned—was commissioned to carrry out the work. This new statue was not subjected to all the mishaps of its predecessor, Lafayette; it was finished without trouble, and the sculptor then went over to select a proper site for his *Liberty enlightening the World.*

A parenthesis: I don't exactly understand the choice of this subject. The New World is said to possess all the liberties, and consequently needs no further enlightening.

I close the parenthesis.

After long examination, M. Bartholdi found at last the desired spot: a magnificent position; a natural pedestal rising from the waters—in short, Bedloe's Island.

" Here it shall stand!" he exclaimed.

He loses no time, hires workmen, and takes them to the island to dig the foundations. While his men were working, the artist was contemplating with emotion the rapidly deepening excavation, beholding in his imagination, and already standing there, the magnificent monument with which his name was to be eternally connected. Suddenly he felt a hand touching him on the shoulder.

The sculptor looks around, and finds himself in presence of a policeman.

"What are you doing there?" the policeman graciously asks.

"I am digging the foundations for *Liberty enlightening the World.*"

"And who has given you permission to dig this hole?"

"Why, it is——"

"You don't know who?"

"Excuse me, sir, it is America herself!—America who has given me an order for a statue, and I was looking for a suitable spot for the erection of the monument; this one is excellent."

"This is all very interesting; but notwithstanding all the liberty that prevails in America, you must learn, sir, that you have no right to dig such a formidable hole without permission; you will please, therefore, follow me to the Mayor."

The laborers, who had stopped work at the sight of the policeman, had already put on their coats, and were about leaving the ground.

"Don't go," shouted the sculptor, in despair; "I shall be back with the authorization in five minutes."

Five minutes!

The artist had not foreseen one thing, nay, several things.

To build on public property without permission is as much an impossibility in the United States as anywhere else.

The Mayor could not take the responsibility upon himself; so he convoked the municipal council. The latter thought the subject too important to be decided without consulting the Governor. The Governor could do nothing without consulting the President of the Republic; the latter could only carry out the decisions of the House of Representatives, which must themselves be approved by the Senate.

Why not do for *Liberty enlightening the World* what was done for the quarantine? Build an island on piles! Here is an idea worthy of the monument. But let the construction be secure, for in case a heavy storm should arise, Bartholdi's island might be set adrift. Who knows where chance might lead it? To the French coast, perhaps, or to Paris, which, in the meantime, might have become a seaport? *

* The accounts of the inauguration of the two statues, recently published in the newspapers, make it unnecessary for the reader to imagine a conclusion to the maestro's humorous chapter.—*French Pub.*

# CHAPTER X.

### LIBERTY IN AMERICA.

AMERICA is indeed the land of liberty!

If you cannot dig a hole without disturbing the whole government hierarchy, you may, however, go where you like, marry whom you please, and eat what you fancy.

There is, however, one melancholy restriction to all this superabundant liberty; you cannot drink what you please every day in the week.

One Sunday, after leading my orchestra with considerable spirit, under a tropical heat, I rushed into a bar for a glass of beer.

The proprietor of the establishment answered with a woful look:

"Impossible, sir; I have no waiters."

"What! no waiters? And what have you done with them all?"

"Every one of them has been arrested for

having insisted upon serving drinks to our customers against the legal prohibition."

"Is it forbidden to drink on Sunday?"

"Strictly forbidden, sir."

"I am going to see about that."

I run to the Brunswick and order boldly:

"A sherry cobbler!"

"I am sorry, sir, to be obliged to disappoint you; the bar is closed, and all my waiters have been arrested."

"But I am dying with thirst."

"The only thing we can give you, sir, is a glass of soda."

Such was, indeed, the state of things in New York. Three hundred waiters had been arrested on that Sunday for carrying refreshments to customers. The customers who called for the drinks may consider themselves lucky enough that they were not arrested themselves.

What a singular liberty!

Nor has anybody the right to hang himself in America.

A drunkard tries to hang himself, but fails, and is brought back to life after a few hours.

When he has recovered his senses he is taken before the judge, who sentences him to six months' imprisonment. Usually it is only three months, but in this case it was an old offender, who had tried it once before. The third time he will be condemned to death. In order to take one's own life the previous authorization of the Governor is required.

Negro emancipation is another grand reform! The dear negroes are free, perfectly free; let me tell you how.

They cannot enter either the cars or any other public conveyances; on no account do the theatres admit them; and if they are received in the restaurants, it is only to wait on the white guests. This is an illustration of Liberty, Equality, and Fraternity.

You think, perhaps, that only negroes are deprived of certain liberties; you are mistaken.

The proprietor of the *Cataract Hotel*, at Niagara Falls, had the following advertisement inserted in the principal daily papers:

"Being a citizen of a perfectly free country,

and having the right to do as I please in my own house, I have decided:

"First and only Article — 'From and after this day, Jews will be excluded from this hotel.'"

It may be interesting to add that after a lapse of two years this liberal hotel-keeper was compelled to give up his establishment for want of business.

The first Sunday I was at leisure after my arrival in Philadelphia, I proposed making a visit to the Exhibition. I found it closed. The exhibitors were restrained from showing their products on Sunday.

I thought of going to the theatre in the evening. Closed too. And the concerts also, just the same as in New York.

Sunday is the only day the working man can call his own. He might avail himself of his few hours of rest for his instruction and recreation, or to improve himself in his calling by the contemplation of the admirable industrial productions which the foremost manufacturers of both hemispheres exhibit here! The exhibition is closed for him. Again, he might seek to refresh his mind by witnessing some play in a good theatre. Yet on this day everything is closed: exhibition, theatres, concerts. If there is any one worthy of respect, it is a working man. After his week's toil he needs one day of mental recreation. He may take his family out, but he cannot enjoy with them the refreshment even of a glass of beer. And what is the consequence? While his wife and children go to church or take a walk, he stops at home and takes to whiskey.

While almost unrestricted liberty is given to industry, invention, and manufactures, the results prove often somewhat inconvenient. If an American conceives an idea, he proceeds at once to carry it out. See, for instance, the rapid development of the cars which have in such a short time driven out the omnibuses. Just now the cars are all the fashion; they are everywhere, and as the streets can only afford space for a limited number, one inventor has imagined to construct elevated railways, and has already commenced the execution of his project. Here is an incident connected with this:

A lady who had just purchased a charming little residence on Broadway, left for the country immediately after, and returned after five or six months to take up her quarters in the new house. Having arrived late at night, she slept soundly. The next morning, a sound like that of thunder, and shrill whistles, suddenly awake her. She runs to the window:

> "Belle sans ornement, dans le simple appareil,
> D'une beauté qu'on vient, d'arracher au sommeil."

She beholds a passing train, with passengers gazing curiously out of every window. She faints.

When she recovered her senses, her first thought, even before closing the window, was to send for a lawyer, and commence a suit for damages against the new company. The house, which had cost her two hundred thousand dollars, was now only worth one quarter of that sum; but she had the privilege of selling it again.

There is one day in the year when the Americans are allowed absolutely unrestricted liberty, the Fourth of July, the anniversary of the national independence. Everything is permitted on this day, and Heaven knows what use and abuse are made of this license! I have preserved a number of the *Courrier des Etats-Unis*, which gives some curious incidents of that memorable day.

Leaving aside many accidents of minor interest, I will confine myself to the more serious casualties. The article is headed: *The Reverse of the Medal.*

"Our first accounts of the casualties and accidents occurring in New York were very incomplete.

"A young girl of nineteen, Mary Henley, residing at No. 261 Sixteenth street, was walking with two of her friends on the Eighth Avenue. Near twenty-second street, fire-crackers were thrown at the girls, in celebration of the glorious day. They paid no attention to it, however, and it was only when they had reached the next block that Mary Henley felt herself burning, and her dress on fire. Terror-stricken, she started running, her clothes ablaze from her head to her feet. The efforts of several men were required to hold her, so agonizing were her pains. The flames were extinguished, but it was too late. Mary Henley was injured beyond possibility of recovery. During the pyrotechnical exhibition in the City Hall Park, a bomb exploded in the midst of a group of spectators: there were five wounded, three of whom are in a dangerous condition.

"Finally, we have before us a list of forty-nine persons, mostly children, wounded during the day or night on the Fourth of July. Some have lost an eye, others a hand; some have had a leg or a rib broken; others the face or other parts of their body badly burned. A few have injured themselves in handling fire-arms, throwing crackers, and falling from roofs and windows. But nine-tenths at least ascribe their wounds to pistol-balls fired by 'unknown persons.' It would only be charitable to believe that these 'unknown persons' were simply awkward fellows.

"These disastrous occurrences are not confined to the city of New York; every large city in the United States suffers from them.

"The celebration of the Centennial in Washington 'was very quiet.' What would have happened had it been more brilliant?

"The rowdy element was very noisy, and four assassinations were committed by drunkards before nightfall.

"Many people visited Washington's tomb at Mount Vernon; unfortunately, even this sacred spot was not free from riot and bloodshed. Several drunken men had a fight with knives. No arrests were made."

In Philadelphia now:

"The Fourth of July was most disastrous for Philadelphia. Besides the conflagration mentioned in another column, which resulted in the death of four persons, this city suffered a ruinous fire, caused by the foolish recklessness with which fire-arms are handled. Boys were firing a cannon near the lumber-yard of Collins & Co., at the foot of Laurel street. A burning piece of wad fell on some shingles, and set fire to them.

"Thus began a fire that destroyed property to the amount of $250,000, and reduced to ashes the whole square situated between the river bank and the east side of Delaware Avenue and Laurel and Shackamaxon streets.

"Every cannon shot may be estimated, on an average, to have caused a similar loss, the most of which falls upon the insurance companies."

These few extracts will give an idea of the number of accidents, fires, and deaths occurring on the Fourth of July in the United States.

As to myself, I am free to confess that these excesses increase greatly my respect for our effete governments, which forbid squarely all liberties that endanger the lives of citizens, and which afford us the protection of our brave gens-d'armes. I have seen unlimited liberty. Thank you! I prefer our sergents-de-ville.

Conclusion:

"The centenary of our independence has been brilliantly celebrated in Detroit," says the *Free Press*, of that city; "every citizen has had his share of it. We will mention, as an instance, the doings of one family—only one of the most respected of the State.

"At six o'clock in the morning, as the head of the family was trying to fasten a flag to the second story window of his house, he fell into the street. He had the misfortune to smash three flower-pots and one of his own ribs. This incident proved the beginning of indescribable disorders. Amid cheers in honor of Independence Day, the neighbors poured lemonade and cognac down his throat; the physicians had a fight about who should take care of him; Mrs. Hamerlin tumbled down the whole length of the back stairs, in her haste to reach the kitchen, where Johnny was exploding crackers in the oven. She arrived all safe, only her cheers for the Fourth of July had to be discontinued until she had recovered her breath. The father and mother being used up, the young Hamerlins proceeded to make the best of it.

"Johnny, greatly disappointed at being unable to fire his crackers in the oven, took half a dozen of them at once in his hands and mouth: off they go, and as a consequence, poor Johnny's mouth will stay shut for a long time.

"The youngest ignited a train of gunpowder and scorched his hands. He went out and got wounded in the leg.

"The girl got a torpedo in the right ear, and a stray bullet missed the left ear.

"In a month from now the whole family shall have recovered, and in the meantime Mr. Hamerlin would not take ten thousand dollars for his Fourth of July fun."

# CHAPTER XI.

### SOCIETIES AND PROCESSIONS.

The Americans have a passion for forming associations, with and without purposes; any pretext is sufficient. The names of all their corporations would fill a volume; the largest are: the Temperance Society, the Free-Masons, the Old-Fellows, the Grand Army of the Republic, etc., etc.

These corporations get up processions for any manifestation they wish to make. Omnibuses, cars, carriages, pedestrians, everything and everybody must stop before their triumphant passage, and they absorb all public attention and curiosity.

Honorary symbols, decorations, ribbons of all colors, and sashes with the most brilliant embroideries (even plumes are to be seen) play the principal part. The Americans like it much, as they can get no Government decorations. In this way some regiments have decorated each other during the civil war.

They have much military music; but what music! My nerves shudder yet!

I saw a procession in Philadelphia. Standards, banners, decorations, carriages, for all the world like the grand march in a fairy play.

One of the bands was made up of at least twelve musicians, who were teazing a lot of cornet à pistons and trombones, marching two by two, the leader in the centre playing the clarionet. Behind him came the triangle and kettledrum.

What amused me most was to notice the fellow who carried the bass drum, and who, while vigorously pounding his instrument, made every effort to maintain it in a horizontal position, in order that every one might have full view of a druggist's advertisement, spread out in fine black letters over the sheepskin.

## CHAPTER XII.

### ADVERTISING AND PUFFING.

The sign on that bass drum leads me to say a word of the system of advertising prevailing in the United States.

It is well known that Americans are fond of advertisements; but it is necessary to travel all over their country, to visit their large cities, their smallest towns, and even the wildest sites, in order to realize to what extent they carry their passion.

I once met in New York two young men walking arm in arm, and on their back was pinned a large placard,

Great Sale of Sewing Machines,
No. 1000 Broadway.

Was it a "sell?" Were these gentlemen really travelling for some house? I rather incline towards the latter hypothesis—at any rate, everybody turned around, laughed, and looked at the sign.

The object was accomplished. Advertisements are to be found everywhere, and of every possible style. Not a flag hanging out of a window but is disfigured with a sign. Streets are here and there crossed by triumphal arches, the only object of which is to give notice of forthcoming sales. The walls are papered with bills of enormous size; mustard manufacturers have their name and address engraved on the very pavements. Cards and circulars are showered in the cars and omnibuses, and numberless hand-bills hang inside.

Sozodont! there is a word I have seen everywhere, and of the meaning of which I am still ignorant. It must certainly be an advertisement. An American would have inquired what it meant. But, like a true Frenchman, I did not feel sufficient interest in the matter to do so.

However, while travelling in the cars, I caught sight of the following words on a telegraph pole: *Only Cure for Rheumatism.* Neither more nor less! Was it because I know so many people afflicted with that disease, or was it on account of the novelty of the advertisement, I know not, but I began, in spite of myself, to watch the telegraph poles. A mile further, I saw it again, but still without any address; further on, the same thing, and so on for some ten miles. On the eleventh I read, to my great delight, the name and address of the advertiser; I came very near purchasing some of his drug as I left the train. The American advertiser plays upon the human brain as a musician does on his piano.

At night, gas, electric light, petroleum, and even magic lanterns are utilized as a means of advertising. Men walk about, inside pasteboard cages lighted inside, and bearing suggestive inscriptions on each of their four faces.

A poor horse falls from fatigue after dragging fifty passengers all day long; at once a boy springs forward and sticks a bill on his nose:

GARGLING OIL.

GOOD FOR MAN AND BEAST.

I found the same advertisement on an almost inaccessible point at Niagara Falls.

This passion for advertisements has been fairly carried beyond the limits of probability. Here is one we find in the newspapers on the subject of a concert at Gilmore's, on the 9th of July:

### Grand Sacred Concert

#### in honor of

### The Emperor of Brazil,

*And last appearance in public of His Majesty Dom Pedro previous to his departure for Europe.*

The words Emperor of Brazil are made very prominent, just as if it were the name of a famous prima donna or a star tragedian.

Imagine, for a moment, the manager stepping before the public and saying: " The Emperor of Brazil, suffering from sudden indisposition, requests your indulgence and relies upon your patience."

Or else:

" The Emperor of Brazil, taken with a sudden

sore throat, begs your pardon, if he cannot appear for the last time this evening," as advertised.

The people would be absolutely entitled to demand their money back.

# CHAPTER XIII.

### THE TURF—JEROME PARK.

I WENT to the races at Jerome Park.

The grounds are a continuation of Central Park, which I have already described, and belong to a wealthy banker, Mr. Belmont.

The reader must not expect me to speak of the *sport* with the wit and *savoir-faire* of my friend Milton, of the *Figaro;* in fact, I hardly know what a starter is. I can only say that I saw in Jerome Park, around a somewhat muddy track, what may be seen on any other race-course. Many horses, many jockeys, many ladies, and many gentlemen. If the horses seemed to me rather large, the jockeys appeared somewhat too lean; but I am not sure. The only thing I can positively assert is that here, as everywhere else, there are always a horse and a jockey who get in first, consequently there are winners who rejoice and losers who grumble. There is betting, as elsewhere.

The public seemed rather lacking in enthusiasm. In France and in England the finish always draws forth cries, shouts, cheers, hurrahs.

For a few seconds every one seems carried away by the excitement of rapid motion, the charm of the spectacle or the expectations of gambling.

Even veteran sportsmen cannot see the decisive moment approaching without manifesting their interest in the struggle in some way, and generally in the most noisy manner. Here, not a sound at the start, and at the finish a mere buzz, at once repressed and followed by impassive silence.

The noise, the bravos, the cheers, which impart such life and animation to Longchamps and Chantilly are wholly wanting in Jerome Park.

As my attention was not entirely occupied by the races, I had ample time to look around me, and I happened to witness a curious and characteristic scene:

In the interval between two races a gentleman was quietly walking up and down on the track, when a thin streak of bluish smoke is suddenly seen arising from his coat-pocket, then growing thicker and becoming at last a dense cloud. The gentleman had an incipient conflagration in his pocket, and the flames now became visible.

"You are on fire!" every one was shouting. He must certainly have felt it by this time, for the flames were already scorching his hips. But, with the coolness of a real Yankee, the gentleman on fire was trying, first of all, to save his pocket-book. Fortunately, just as he drew it from the depths of his jacket, some policemen had already got hold of him and were tearing off his burning garment. He walked off in his shirt sleeves, as cool as ever, thanking the public and the policemen with a grateful glance.

I had already had occasion to admire the elegant dresses of the American ladies; this day my impression became even more established. They wore at the races their freshest and brightest toilets.

Embellished by the presence of all these elegant creatures, the view of the race-course was simply lovely.

While acknowledging, with pleasure, the excellent taste of American ladies, I regret being unable to say as much of the gentlemen.

They dress generally very plainly, and even negligently. At the theatres and concerts, you see them wearing those horrid suits, all of the same material, which we hardly ever venture upon, except in the country, or at the watering places. Low-crowned hats and soft hats are much worn, and the most distinguished gentlemen do not hesitate to escort, in this plight, the most exquisitely-dressed ladies to a party or a dinner. *Per contra*, many wear white neckties at all times of day and night, and the contrast between this ceremonious article of dress and the rest of the costumes is very strange indeed.

Something rather surprising for strangers is to see that all Americans have, near the waist, and beneath the skirts of their coats, a rather marked protuberance. This is caused by the revolver which they generally carry in that locality, in a pocket specially made for the purpose.

## CHAPTER XIV.

#### THE AMERICAN NEWSPAPER PRESS.

NEWSPAPERS have in New York a far greater importance than in Europe.

It must not be taken for granted that the press in the New World is also free too.

While in Europe the governments watch and control the newspapers, here the religious sects and political associations perform this duty quite efficiently.

The editors, it must be confessed, submit readily to this servitude, and make the best of it.

Being familiar with the principal establishments of the French press, I naturally wished to visit those of the leading New York papers.

New York editors are better off than ours in regard to space.

Imagine immense establishments, vast buildings, and inside these palaces of the American press a continual going and coming, and the activity of a bee-hive.

The journals of New York have, like those of Paris, located themselves in the busiest part of the city. In order to secure prompt and reliable information, a newspaper should be placed in the midst of a business centre.

It is on Broadway, therefore, that the offices of the representative American press are to be found.

There is no dfficulty in finding these. If it is in day-time, walk boldly in the tallest building; you will be sure to be right. The New York Tribune building, for instance, is nine stories high.

If it is at night, open your eyes; the most brilliantly illuminated edifice is sure to be the very one you are looking for. Behind those shining panes the journalists are at work. They say sometimes, figuratively, in France, that a newspaper is a light-house; in America it would be a literal fact.

The offices are most complete and comfortable. A telegraph, like the one already mentioned, is here continually at work. The composing, stereotyping, and press rooms are admirably equipped with improved machinery and appliances.

Here are now some particulars about the leading New York journals:

The first is the *New York Herald*, founded some thirty years ago by Mr. James Gordon Bennett.

Its present circulation is about 70,000 copies. Each number contains, according to want, eight, sixteen, and even twenty-four pages.

In size, it is about one-quarter larger than the Paris papers.

Small types being generally used in America, it is easy to see how much news, editorial matter, and advertisements can be crowded in an average number of the *New York Herald*. To speak only of advertisements, there are twenty-eight columns of them, during the dull season. In lively times, the number of columns reaches sixty. The price of a single insertion varies from twenty-five cents to one dollar.

Its advertising patronage, copious news, and

vast circulation, make of the *New York Herald* the leading newspaper of the United States. The *personnel* required for such an administration is, of course, enormous. Seventy compositors, twenty pressmen, twenty office clerks, and a legion of boys. So much for the manual labor, without counting an army of carriers and venders.

The editorial staff of the *New York Herald* is scattered over all parts of the globe. Among its oldest contributors I may mention Mr. Connery, a musical critic of great abilty.

To Mr. Bennett, Jr., I have devoted a place among my portraits. He is at once proprietor and manager of the establishment, and, without doubt, the most interesting personage in it.

Next to the *Herald* comes the *New York Times*, which prints 40,000 numbers daily. It is remarkable for the influence which its opinions and literary authority exercise on the public. It was founded by Messrs. Raymond, Jones, and Wesley.

Mr. Raymond, a distinguished statesman, retained the chief editorship until his death, and was succeded by Mr. Jennings, of the *London Times*. The present principal proprietor is Mr. Jones, a man of great personal influence. He upholds firmly the reputation of the establishment, and under his vigilant management it ranks all other American papers in point of purity and elegance. The chief editor is Mr. Ford, a talented writer. Mr. Schwab writes the critiques on music and the drama. They are both men whose merit and ability are fully equal to their respective duties. The *New York Times* uses Walker presses, which require only two men to work them, and print from 15,000 to 17,000 copies per hour.

The *New York Tribune*, founded by Horace Greeley, an eminent philanthropist and writer, and most decided abolitionist. He was a candidate for the Presidency in 1872, but was defeated. He died of grief and disappointment shortly after.

This journal advocates the theories of modern reformers, including women's rights. Mr. Jay Gould, formerly Fisk's partner, is the proprietor. The paper is well written, but seems to have lost some of its former influence. Mr. Winter, an excellent and amiable writer, is the dramatic critic. Mr. Hassard is the musical critic, and a fanatic admirer of Wagner.

The *World.* Democratic organ. 12,000 to 15,000 numbers daily. The chief editor, Mr. Hurlbut, has travelled and seen much. He is an accomplished gentleman and a writer of talent. The inconsistency of his political opinions is sometimes criticised by his fellow-journalists. But is this really a fault nowadays? The musical critic, Mr. Wheeler, is a brilliant *feuilletoniste.*

The *Sun,* average daily circulation 120,000 copies, sells for two cents. Editor and principal proprietor, Mr. Dana, a first-class journalist, who speaks all languages, and excels in condensing the news and unearthing scandals.

The *Evening Post,* Republican. Large circulation. The editor, Mr. William Cullen Bryant, is a well-known American poet.

The *Evening Telegram,* published by the *New York Herald.* This paper differs from all the others in this, that it is a sort of continuous publication. It is always being set up, always in press, always selling. A dispatch is received; quick, an edition is struck off, and as dispatches keep coming all day . . . . .

*Le Courrier des Etats-Unis* (French); an excellent paper, founded forty years ago. The journal is edited with praiseworthy care and holds a prominent position among foreign publications. Mr. Frédéric Gaillardet, to whom it owes its first prosperity, sold it to Mr. Charles Lasalle, the present proprietor. Mr. Léon Meunier, his son-in-law and partner, is the chief editor. Mr. Charles Villa is the critic.

*Le Messager Franco-Americain* (French); ultra Rebublican; established ten years ago. Mr. De Mavil, proprietor. Mr. Louis Cortambert, chief editor.

The *Staats-Zeitung* (German) prints 25,000 to 30,000 copies daily. An ably written and accomplished journal, of great political influence in New York. It is located in a fine building, opposite the *Times*, which its manager, Mr. Oswald Ottendorfer, has erected. He is an

Austrian by birth; but has resided in America some twenty-five years. He is an active politician and able writer. The founder of the journal was Mrs. Uhl, a woman of rare energy. The beginning was somewhat rough. Like Mr. Bennett, the lady-editor often, at first, delivered the papers herself to her subscribers.

The Associated Press answers to our Agence-Havas.

The Reporters' Association deserves a special mention. Members of the craft, representing all the papers, have formed a sort of partnership, for the purpose of procuring and communicating to each other all accounts of accidents, crimes, etc. A certain number attend at police head-quarters, whence, in case of any event of note, they may be called by telegraph. A few take charge of the civil courts. Some fifteen meet every morning at the office of the paper, and are dispatched by the news-editor to the different wards. They all understand short-hand and telegraphing.

By means of a telegraph instrument, they are able to report events which have occurred a a thousand miles away, so that the paper may publish five or six columns on the subject of a crime or an accident the very morning after its occurrence.

# CHAPTER XV.

### A FEW CHARACTER SKETCHES.

Up to this time I have spoken principally of manners and things in America. When I have had to bring a personage before the public, I have generally made use of an impersonal designation. I mentioned, for instance, that I had seen, in such a place, "*an odd character*," in such another, "*a pretty woman.*" In order to give my readers a more complete and more perfect idea of Americans, I will now endeavor to sketch a few pen-portraits.

I only wish that this gallery of contemporary pictures may afford as much gratification to the readers of this book as I derived myself from personal intercourse with the originals.

### MR. BENNETT.

Mr. Bennett is the son of the celebrated James

Gordon Bennett, who founded the *New York Herald* some thirty years ago. The *New York Herald* yields an income of two million francs a year.

To state how much work, perseverance, and genius were brought to bear in order to accomplish this result would require more than one volume, and I know of no one who could faithfully translate such a book except, perhaps, the founder of the French *Figaro*. I have often wondered what would have happened if my illustrious friend H. de Villemessant and Mr. James Gordon Bennett had met in 1848, and what kind of a journal would have been produced by the combined enterprise of the two men who have best understood the men and things of their time.

Upon reflection it is fortunate that chance did not bring them together. Villemessant would have retained James Gordon Bennett at any price and by every possible means. Paris would doubtless have benefited by such a measure, but New York would have lost much.

Mr. Bennett, Jr., is thirty years of age, and sharing the good fortune of hereditary monar chies, he is in all respects the worthy successor of his father.

His appearance is that of a perfect gentleman; he is tall, of a dark, pale complexion, and is distinguished looking. Like all men who work much and own much property, he seems cold and reserved, save when animated by some sudden impression. The proprietor of the *Herald* is certainly conscious that he holds a high position; he commands an army of faithful correspondents, bold and devoted, always ready at a moment's notice to rush from one end of the world to the other. He has throughout the world as many agents as a great power has consuls, and the letters and dispatches which he receives or sends daily are numbered by thousands. Thus no event of any importance occurs in either hemisphere without it being related in his journal a few hours after.

It was Mr. Bennett who scattered a million to obtain news of the unfortunate Livingstone, and every one remembers the sympathizing curiosity which accompanied his reporter, Mr. Stanley, who, starting with a hundred others, had the good fortune of first reaching the goal.

His remarkable talent for doing things on a large scale increases daily the reputation of his journal.

In the midst of so numerous and absorbing occupations, Mr. Bennett is yet able to find time for pleasure. He is fond of Paris, which he visits frequently; he speaks French like a resident of the Boulevard de la Madelaine. One day he took a fancy to go to England in a yacht, upon which Mr. Batbie would certainly not have ventured to sneeze. This fancy trip made a great stir in the world, and had its imitators; two other yachts started at the same time; bets were made, and, as usual, the hero of the *Herald* arrived before the others. Mr. Bennett is fond of social intercourse, and entertains with an extravagance which reminds one of the happy days of the great lords of the last century. On one of his estates he has a model stud, and he often gets up races, to which he invites all the *gentlemen riders* of the United States. The attraction of these races is that the master of the house supplies the horses, and that the gentleman who wins takes away his horse, as in our chateaux the sportsmen carry away the traditional hamper of game. Add to all this, most graceful manners, and you will even then form but a faint idea of one of the most interesting personages of the New World.

### THE MANAGER MAURICE GRAU.

Quite a young man, scarcely twenty-eight years old, but looking forty. Incessant work, care of all sort, an extraordinary activity, and continual preoccupations have made him look prematurely old. He has led a busy life, an existence more feverish, more consuming in America than anywhere else. He has already made and lost five or six fortunes. One day he is worth millions, and the next he has not a penny. Nor is this very strange, for Maurice Grau often manages five theatres at one and the same time; an Italian opera in New York, a French theatre in Chicago, a music-hall in San Francisco, an English dramatic theatre in Havana, and a Spanish comic opera in Mexico.

It is he who brought Rubenstein, the famous

pianist, to America. What a campaign that was. Two hundred concerts in less than six months; sometimes two concerts a day.

At present Maurice Grau manages Mlle. Aimée's troupe. It is he who made the agreement with Rossi. The Italian tragedian is expected in two months, and will travel a year with his clever impresario.

### THE ORCHESTRA LEADER, THOMAS.

Thomas, a violinist, and, according to report, a very ordinary violinist in the New York opera, soon perceived that his position did not pay. He gave up the bow and took up the leader's baton. To distinguish himself from others who beat time, he had the sense to create a specialty, by making himself the propagator of the Wagner music, which has procured him a well-established artistic reputation. He is still a young man. To do him justice, he has formed an excellent orchestra. To accomplish that object he has adopted the right means; cost what it may, he engages the best musicians in America, and continues to pay them a high price. Wherever he goes, and whatever he undertakes, he can always rely upon the assistance of twelve first-rate performers, who never desert him. Thus his orchestra is noted, among all others, for its wonderful *ensemble*. As leader, Thomas did not appear to me fully up to the reputation he enjoys. He does not lead with spirit. I have seen him at the head of his musicians interpret the music of Rossini, Auber, Verdi, Hérold, without force or animation. When by chance he attempts to display a little energy, he leads with both arms at once, which makes him look from behind like a huge bird about to take its flight. He has a great partiality for the music of the director of the Conservatoire of Paris, our excellent friend Ambroise Thomas. He seldom fails to place on his programme a piece written by the author of *Mignon*. The public generally believes that it is the leader Thomas who is entitled to credit for the piece. If Thomas is not a leader of the first order, he is nevertheless a man of real merit. Great praise is due to him for having selected his orchestra so well, and for having done so much to popularize classic music in America.

### MARETZEK.

A Hungarian from Vienna, born in Italy, an old resident of New York. About fifty years old—an intelligent, open, and witty countenance. A character for which Americans have much sympathy. At times manager, at others leader of the orchestra, he has originated almost every company which have played Italian opera in the United States. When the business of manager fares badly, which sometimes happens, he turns orchestra leader. Scarcely, however, is he leader than, as he is much liked, funds come in and enable him to form another company, and try his luck once more. I cannot say whether he is a good manager, as I have never seen him at work, but he is an excellent leader, and composes also charming music. At present Maretzek is directing the concerts at *Offenbach Garden* in Philadelphia. You may be sure that before three months he will have laid down his baton to undertake some theatrical enterprise or other.

### WEBER.

Weber is a German, naturalized American.

He has lived for twenty years in America. I visited the workshops where he manufactures his pianos. The installation is magnificent. The master of the house received me very graciously. He is a very agreeable man, with a prepossessing face, frank and open. I am not aware whether he be descended from his famous namesake, Charles Marie Von Weber. I forgot to ask him. However that may be, as the composer was master in his art, the American Weber is master in his. The instruments of his manufacture are much sought after in the United States.

### MISS ESMERALDA CERVANTES.

A young and charming person, who travels in both hemispheres with her harp. As musician, she has great talent; she has but one fault—that of putting all her titles on her visiting card—and certainly she has enough of them. I copy verbatim:

### ESMERALDA CERVANTES.

Harpist to the royal and imperial courts of S. M. doña Isabella II., of S. M. don Alfonso XII., of S. M. don Louis I., and of S. M. don Pedro II., of Brazil. Honorary citizen of the Republic of Uruguay, decorated with several crosses and medals; honorary professor of the Conservatory of Barcelona; president of the lyric Esmeralda of Spain; of the singing societies, Euterpe, Montevideo, and Esmeralda of Buenos-Ayres; of the lyric society *la Balma*; of the oriental hospital and of the benevolent society of Buenos-Ayres; honorary member of the singing society, Euterpe of Barcelona, and of the society of the *Torre*, of the same city; of the philharmonic society of Brazil; of the Lyra of Montevideo; of the literary circles and of the *Union of Lima*; of the benevolent societies of *Beneficiencia*; of the society of *Caridad*; of the Spanish hospital and of the society of *Misericorde* of Buenos-Ayres; of the *Beneficiencia* of Rosario and of Valparaiso; of the *Beneficiencia España* of Lima; *member of the society of Firemen of Callao*; protectress of the society of ladies of the *Buen Pastor* in America and Europe.

Let us add that Miss Esmeralda Cervantes is scarcely sixteen years old! What will she be when she is thirty?

### MORA.

Mora is the head of a superb photographic establishment. He has the most agreeable class of customers imaginable. Before his objective-glasses the prettiest American ladies come to sit. They are right, for were it possible to do so,

Mora is skilful enough to render them prettier still.

### MARA.

A minature painter. He has a talent for coloring photographs, and making real miniatures of them.

### A SENATOR.

I met in New York a personage who, starting from the lowest strata, has reached the rank of senator by the strength of his muscle. This is not a figure of speech. A simple workman at first, and gifted with herculean strength, he left the workshop to become a pugilist, and from the prize-ring he stepped into political life. John Morrissey is still a young man, tall and splendidly proportioned. His nose is slightly broken; it is, I am told, a glorious souvenir of a memorable encounter with another boxer.

After earning some money by fighting against the "Bulwarks of Cincinnati," and the terrible " Bruisers of Chicago," the pugilist retired and opened two gambling-houses, one in New York, the other in Saratoga. Fortune comes quickly in enterprises of this kind, and the former champion is now worth a formidable amount of dollars. Having acquired popularity, as well as a considerable fortune, he had no difficulty in getting into the Senate. After reading the preceding account, you may perhaps imagine that this senator must have retained a certain roughness or brutality in his manners. You are entirely mistaken. He is, on the contrary, a very gentle distinguished man, conversing on all subjects with much tact and intelligence.

In France, Harpin, known as the *Bulwark of Lyons*, would have considerable difficulty, notwithstanding the eccentricity of the times, to reach a parliamentary situation. But the devil does not lose much for all that; for more than once our Assemblies have been transformed into arenas, in which the struggle was not always the most courteous.

# CHAPTER XVI.

### PHILADELPHIA.

HERE I am in Philadelphia. It is eleven o'clock at night. I put up at the Continental Hotel, a reproduction, as regards size, of the Fifth Avenue Hotel at New York. There are, however, even more people than usual; for the Americans give a dinner to-day to the Emperor of Brazil, who is staying at the hotel. From my apartment I hear a band of music, not entirely harmonious, which is playing *Orphée aux Enfers*. Are they saluting the departure of Dom Pedro, or my own arrival?—it is, perhaps, for both, unless the music has been ordered, which is most probable, to play during dinner.

The next day, at ten o'clock, I went down to the dining-room for breakfast. It was a repetition of the New York meal. There is, however, one thing which gives a peculiar and curious appearance to the room; it is that all the waiters are negroes or mulattoes. To be received as waiter in this hotel, it is necessary to have a coating of liquid blacking on your face. The dining-room is immense, and it is a curious sight to see about thirty tables of different sizes, chiefly occupied by pretty women in elegant dresses, around which some forty or fifty negroes are skipping about. The negroes are not bad-looking, but the mulattoes have magnificent heads. I have an idea that Alexandre Dumas must have passed some time in this country; for the portrait of our great novelist is reproduced here to perfection.

As soon as I had breakfasted I started for the Exhibition, for I had forgotten that it was Sunday. On Sunday the Exhibition is closed; the houses and taverns are closed; everything is closed in this joyous city; it is exceedingly gay. The few people that one meets are coming from church, with their Bibles and funeral faces. Should you be guilty of smiling, they look at you with horror; should you laugh, they would have you arrested.

The streets are very fine, and wide enough to

rival the Boulevard Haussman. On both sides are houses of red brick, with window-frames in white marble; here and there pretty little mansions; but the churches are very numerous. The pretty women of Philadelphia probably require much praying for, and I see no great harm in the fact.

A new City Hall is being built, in white marble, and will cost two hundred million of francs.

My two friends and I did not know how on earth to spend our Sunday. We were advised to go to Indian Rock, in Fairmount Park. It takes two hours to go there, but the park is endless.

The people of Philadelphia are proud of this immense garden, and with reason, for it is impossible to imagine anything finer or more picturesque. Here and there are little cottages nestling in the shrubbery; small streams winding under the trees, green valleys, shady ravines, splendid woods; it is magnificent.

From time to time one sees a tavern, a public-house full of people. The men, according to the American fashion, stretched in rocking-chairs, or on ordinary chairs, resting their feet upon some object higher than their heads. They all had large glasses of red, green, or yellow lemonade before them. Strong drinks are forbidden—on Sunday one must confine himself to mild drinks. The law cannot be the same for all, for a carriage, driven by two residents of the place, quite drunk (and I hardly suppose the lemonade could have produced this effect), nearly ran into ours several times. These questionable observers of the Sunday law passed us several times, and seemed bent upon upsetting us. On reaching Indian Rock, our coachman gravely dismounted from his box, and took hold of the reins of the horse driven by the two drunken men. He begged these gentlemen to get out of their carriage. On their refusal, a policeman gravely got into their carriage, lifted out one of them, handing him over into the arms of another policeman, who received him with the greatest politeness; he then gravely took the reins and drove off with the other. A dozen words were not exchanged between them; all was done silently, gravely, methodically.

# CHAPTER XVII.

### OFFENBACH GARDEN.

THE establishment where I was to give concerts was a covered garden, recently built on the model of Gilmore's Garden, but smaller. The same stage, the same cascade, the same Niagara, the same colored glasses, the same rustic boxes. What pleased me most was that I had at Philadelphia almost the same musicians as at New York; they were less numerous it is true—seventy-five instead of one hundred and ten—the hall not being so large. My permission had been asked to call it *Offenbach Garden*, and I could not refuse. *Offenbach Garden* was as favorable to me as Gilmore Garden. The same enthusiasm; the same *encores;* the same brilliant concerts. The day after each concert the journals overwhelmed me with praise; once only a journal made me a reproach, which caused me much grief. Speaking of my personal appearance, dress coat, black trousers, white cravat, the critic observed that I wore gray gloves. The observation was correct; I must humbly admit that I have worn white gloves four times only in my life; once as groomsman, another time on my wedding day, and the two others at the marriage of my two daughters.

On Sundays, concerts, as well as all other amusements, are forbidden. One day the proprietor of the garden came to tell me that he had obtained permission to give a sacred concert.

"I rely upon you," he said; "I have already had the bills printed. See!"

He showed me the placard, which I copy faithfully for the benefit of the reader, on the opposite page.

OFFENBACH GARDEN

COR BROAD AND CHERRY STS

SUNDAY EVENING, JUNE 25 TH

AT 8 O'CLOCK P. M.,

# GRAND
# SACRED
# CONCERT

BY

# M. OFFENBACH

AND THE

GRAND ORCHESTRA

IN A CHOICE SELECTION OF

SACRED AND CLASSICAL MUSIC

ADMISSION,            50 CENTS

LEDGER JOB PRINT. PHILAD'

For a whole week my *Grand Sacred Concert* was placarded all over the town, and during this time I prepared a very pretty programme:

> *Deo gratias*, from the Domino noir.
> *Ave Maria*, by Gounod.
> *Religious March*, from la Haine.
> *Ave Maria*, by Schubert.
> *Litanie de la Belle Hélène*, dis-moi, Vénus.
> *Hymn*, from Orphée aux Enfers.
> *Prayer*, from the Grande Duchesse (Dites-lui).
> *Seraphic Dance*, Burlesque Polka.
> *Angelus*, from the Mariage aux Lanternes.

Unfortunately the authorities changed their mind at the last moment. I regret that the affair did not take place, for I am persuaded that my *Sacred Concert* would have been a great success.

# CHAPTER XVIII.

### ON THE WAY TO NIAGARA—PULLMAN CARS.

THE road from New York to Niagara is very fine. The landscape, as far as Albany, is truly marvellous along the splendid river Hudson. I do not know to what river in Europe I could compare the American river. There are places which remind me of the most beautiful parts of the Rhine; there are others which surpass in beauty all that I had ever seen. The voyage is made in the most agreeable manner; the Pullman cars are a precious institution. The great problem is realized by these wonderful carriages of being on a railway and having none of the unpleasantness of travelling by rail. One is not, as with us, packed in narrow compartments, nor exposed to the tingling sensation which passes in one's limbs after some hours of immobility. One has not to fear ankylosis of the fatigued limbs from keeping the same position for too great a length of time. In the American train you can walk about from one car to another all the way from the baggage-car to the buffer of the last carriage. When tired of walking, you can rest in an elegant saloon, upon excellent arm-chairs. You have at hand all necessary comforts to make life agreeable. I cannot better sum up my admiration for American railways than by saying that they are really—a cradle on wheels.

I do not, however, like the continual bell which accompanies you all along the journey with its funeral knell; but it is, perhaps, only a matter of habit, and one should not have too delicate an ear when travelling in America, for one is constantly persecuted by unpleasant sounds.

At Utica, where we stopped a few minutes to lunch, I .saw (and heard, alas!) a large negro beating a tam-tam. He was evidently playing music of his own composing, for he beat sometimes loud and with astonishing quickness, sometimes with measured slowness. I forgot to lunch while watching this peculiar musician. During his last piece of music—for so he doubtless considered it—I was all ears and eyes. He began by a *fortissimo* which deafened you, for the negro was a powerful fellow, and applied all his strength. After this brilliant opening, his music continued *decrescendo, piano, pianissimo,* then silence.

At the same moment the train started. I had just time to jump on, and we were again at full speed.

At Albany we stopped to dine. I found another great negro before the hotel, who resembled the first, and who was also playing the tam-tam. This must certainly be a country exceedingly fond of the tam-tam.

A hungry belly has no ears, says the proverb. I am grieved in this case at being unable to agree with the wisdom of nations, for, notwithstanding my appetite, the negro's music tormented me during all the meal. He played exactly like his colleague at Utica—the same repetition of *forte, piano,* and *pianissimo.* I was on the point of asking if the negroes really considered the solo on the tam-tam to be music, and if this was their national air, when one of my friends addressed me.

"This negro puzzles you," he said; "you will see one just like him at every station on the line."

"Is it an attention on the part of the company?" I asked.

"No, it is the hotel-keepers who engage them. The negroes play all the time the train is at the station; their music warns the travellers who are inside the hotel. While the tam-tam is loud, you can remain quiet; when the sound decreases, you had better hurry; when it is at the lowest, the travellers know that they must jump into the cars, which, like Louis XIV., do not wait, and, worse still, give no warning. So much the worse for those who lose the train."

I do not know whether I prefer the American style to that employed by the hotel-keeper at Morcenz, between Bordeaux and Biarritz. Having no negro, the landlord himself shouts, in a stentorian voice: "Five minutes more! four minutes more! three minutes more!"

The two systems are alike; the only difference is that one deafens you with his voice inside the establishment, while the other stuns you with his music in the open air.

# CHAPTER XIX.

### THE FALLS OF NIAGARA.

Much has been written on the subject of this wonderful waterfall, but no one has yet been able to describe the impression produced by the sight of the great stream at the moment when it leaps headlong, from a height of a hundred and fifty feet, into the fathomless abyss beneath. The view of that vast amphitheatre, of that prodigious volume of water, breaking into foam, with a roar of thunder, like the huge tidal wave that follows an earthquake, made me giddy, and caused me to forget all I had ever read, all I had ever heard, and all that had ever suggested itself to my imagination. This diluvial torrent, framed within the wildest scenery, surrounded by lofty trees of the deepest green, upon which a shower of spray is constantly falling like perpetual dew, defies photography, painting, or description. In order to describe, there must be some point of comparison. To what can Niagara be compared, that unrivalled, everlasting phenomenon, to the magnificence of which we can never become accustomed!

While we were absorbed in the contemplation of this wonder—

"This is the spot," said our guide, "where an Indian met with his fate a fortnight ago. Carried away by the current, the slight craft that held him was drawing near to the Falls, notwithstanding all his efforts. The Indian, feeling his strength giving way, saw that he was lost. He ceased to struggle, wrapped himself up in his red blanket as in a shroud, and laid himself down in the bottom of his boat. A few seconds after he was on the crest of the gigantic wave, and was shot with the rapidity of lightning into this watery grave, covered with a mist of immaculate white."

After hearing the story of this catastrophe, so fearful, yet so grand, I could not help envying the fate of the unfortunate red-skin, and I wondered that all Americans in distress did not prefer the Falls of Niagara to the insipid revolver. After having long enjoyed this wonderful spectacle, I crossed the bridge and set foot on Canadian soil. Here, I had been told, I would see Indians. I expected to find savages, and was surprised to find only dealers in bric-à-brac. They were hideous, I confess; they looked quite ferocious, I admit also: but I doubt whether they were genuine Indians. However that may be, they surrounded me on all sides, offered me bamboos, fans, cigar-holders, and pocket-books of a doubtful taste. They reminded me of the Indians of the forest of Fontainbleau who sell pen-holders and paper-knives.

Nevertheless, I made a few purchases; but I verily believe that I brought back into France some curiosities which had been procured at the selling out of some Parisian bazar.

# CHAPTER XX.

### THE DAUPHIN ELEAZAR.

On the boat that takes you to all the fine parts of the lake is a distributor of hand-bills, who compels you to take his little paper. In Paris, when one of these persons offers you a bill, you take it to encourage business, but you manage to throw it away ten steps further. I had the good idea not to treat thus the prospectus which had been handed me, and I had my reward; for the paper which had been almost forced upon me is a valuable document, which may have the greatest influence upon the destiny of France. This document begins, it is true, by explaining, like an ordinary guide-book, the beauties of the various places to be seen on the borders of the lake; but it contains an extremely curious pas age, which I am happy to give here verbatim:

"Howe Point, near the outlet of the lake, is named in honor of the idol of the army, Lord Howe, who was killed at this place in the first engagement with the French. Here it was that *Louis XVI.*, of France, through the instrumentality of two French priests, in 1795, banished his son, *the Royal Dauphin*, when but seven years old, and arranged with an Indian chief, one Thomas Williams, to adopt him as his own son. He received the name of Eleazar, and afterwards, as the Rev. Eleazar Williams, was educated and ordained to the ministry, officiating for many years among the Oneidas of Western New York, and afterwards in Wisconsin, where he was visited, a few years since, by the *Prince de Joinville*, and offered large estates in France, if he would renounce his rights to the THRONE OF FRANCE. These tempting offers he declined, preferring to retain his right as KING OF FRANCE, although he might spend his life in preaching the gospel to the poor savages, which he did until the time of his death, some years since."

After having read this narration, as touching as it was probable, I made inquiries, and learnt that the Rev. Dauphin Eleazar had left a son.

Another claimant!

Imagine this gentleman arriving in France. What a complication! I tremble to think of it.

## CHAPTER XXI.

#### THE RETURN FROM NIAGARA—SLEEPING-CARS.

ON the way from Niagara I took the night train. I was glad of an opportunity to try in person the sleeping-cars of which I had heard so much.

I entered the car, which seemed arranged, as usual, with large easy-chairs on each side of the passage-way—special rooms for smokers, and all the convenience which I had so much admired on my first trip. Nothing indicated, in the arrangement of the cars, that one could sleep there in a bed, and I began to believe in some mystification, so utterly impossible did it seem that all the ladies and gentlemen who sat in this fine saloon could be supplied with sleeping accommodations.

Nevertheless, at about nine o'clock, when it began to get quite dark, two servants of the company appeared and commenced the arrangements. In the twinkling of an eye our seats were transformed into beds, and in the most simple manner. Upon the seats joined together by a board, they placed first a mattress, sheets, and blankets. The saloon, thus turned into a dormitory, would not have been sufficient for the number of travellers without another expedient. Above each of the beds is a little apparatus, which drops down, and which proves to be a sort of folding-bed. There are thus two stories of beds in each compartment—the ground floor and the entresol. But, before retiring, there is a preliminary operation, which people are not generally fond of performing in public. The men, were they alone, could easily undress before each other; but the ladies, it will readily be understood, cannot undress before all the travellers. The inventor of the sleeping-cars was therefore obliged to find some means of reassuring the modesty of the fair sex. This he has succeeded in doing by making of each pair of beds—the upper and the lower ones—a complete bed-room. Two large curtains, drawn parallel the whole length of the car, form a long corridor in the centre, in which the travellers can walk, if so disposed. Between each of these curtains and the side of the wagon are smaller curtains. A person in bed is thus in a little room, which at the head has a wooden wall, and on the three other sides a curtain partition. I have known hotels where the walls were less discreet than those of the sleeping-car.

All the preparations being finished, an amusing scene begins. Each one chooses his bed, and selects the little compartment which appears most advantageous to him. Then for some minutes is heard in the adjoining rooms the noise of boots falling on the floor, or the pleasant rustling sound which reveals the removing of a skirt.

When a husband travels with his wife, he has a perfect right to occupy the same compartment with her. This fact was revealed to me by an extremely interesting conversation, held in a low tone, which took place in the next berth to mine on the right side. However discreet one may be, one is always a little curious to know what neighbors, chance has given you. On the left, the occupant of the cabin was a charming young lady. She had retired to her room as soon as the transformation of the saloon had taken place, and, to her honor be it said, her presence was revealed only by the most discreet motions. Then when the curtain ceased to stir, the sound of a bed receiving a light body informed me that she had at last lain down for the night. A few minutes elapsed. I had also stretched myself upon my bed, but not being accustomed to this kind of travelling hotel, and being kept awake by my old Parisian habit of going to sleep very late, I lay with my eyes open, thinking of the strange aspect of this American dormitory. In the passage at my feet, formed by the two long curtains of which I have spoken, I heard the sound of people walking to and fro. Who could they be ? I cast a glance upon the corridor, and saw—*horresco referens*—ladies in night jackets (it is true they were not the prettiest) who were going . . . I know not where. I saw also a good-looking Yankee who came out of his room. After ascertaining that the road was clear, he walked to the platform and lit a cigar.

A moment later he threw away his fragrant Havana, and returned inside the car; but instead of going straight to his cabin, he directed his steps—you have already guessed—to that of my pretty neighbor on the left.

His irruption into the sanctuary of the pretty American lady provoked a series of exclamations, uttered in a low voice, so as not to arouse the general attention of the dormitory, and the invader retired, making some excuse for his mistake. The night passed without any further incident.

Scarcely had rosy-fingered morn appeared, than the servants appeared also. Ladies and gentlemen tumbled out of their beds, and made their toilets as best they could behind their respective curtains. The agents of the company then restored everything to its usual order in the twinkling of an eye. After our night's sleep, therefore, we met again in the saloon as fresh and as well as though we had spent the night in a hotel.

In Albany an American presented me to his wife and mother-in-law. While we were talking, a pedlar came along with fans, and I bought two for a few cents and offered them to the ladies.

"We accept, sir," they said, "but on one condition."

"What is that?" I inquired.

"That you write your name on a corner of the fan."

"Oh! an autograph," I said, at once complying with their desire.

I noticed, on several occasions, what a mania Americans have for autographs. It is a passion which they carry to a point of being indiscreet.

I received, on an average, during my stay in the States, about ten requests a day, coming from all parts of the American territory. I have been hailed, followed, and dogged in hotels, public gardens, theatres, and even in the street, by determined collectors, who insisted upon having a few lines of my handwriting. My calligraphy was at a premium, and I received letters of every kind, some simple, others ingenious:

"SIR,—I have made a bet with one of my friends that you were born in Paris. As the amount is considerable, will you kindly drop me a line and let me know if I have won?"

Another had wagered that I had originally come from Cologne; a third affirmed that my native place was the little German town of Offenbach, famous for its manufacture of cutlery; and all ended with the same request for *a line*.

Some of my unknown correspondents proceeded in another manner:

"My name is Michel; I am a distant relative of your brother-in-law, Robert. Send me a line, and let me know how he is."

These were not aware even that Mitchel and Michel were not spelled alike.

There was also the following model:

"Sir,—I have something very important to communicate to you. Will you admit me? Please send a line in reply."

I could mention forty or fifty of the same kind.

One day an Englishman addressed me, while I was dining at the Brunswick.

"I live at San Francisco," he said, "and I should like to have your name."

My dinner was about over; I rose, gave him my

card, and left him a little disappointed. I imagined that I had done with the fellow; but the next day he was waiting for me, and, as I entered the dining-room, he rushed to me, with paper, pen, and ink in his hand.

"Just your signature!" he said, in a tremulous voice; "I start this evening; it would give me so much pleasure; I have come from such a distance."

It was impossible to refuse a man who had come from so far.

All the requests I received invariably contained an envelope, directed and stamped, and I accumulated five or six hundred of these. I hereby inform my fair applicants for autographs that I carefully collected their stamps, disposed of them, and sent the product to a charitable institution.

Let them receive, then, with the assurance of my profound regret, the thanks of the poor.

## CHAPTER XXII.

#### THE MISERIES OF A MUSICIAN.

Besides the concerts which I had engaged to direct, I had promised Mdlle. Aimée to lead at some of the representations which she intended giving in America. According to my promise, I had held the baton of leader of the orchestra in New York, at the theatre where Mdlle. Aimée sang. I thought I had thus discharged my obligation towards her; but when my series of concerts were over in Philadelphia, she came to inform me that she was about starting for Chicago, and begged me to lead a last representation at X——. I have special reasons for not giving the name of the town. I intended myself going to Chicago, and X—— being on the way, I consented. I reached X—— early in the morning. The piece for the evening was *La Belle Parfumeuse*. I went to the theatre, so as to have at least one rehearsal with my orchestra.

I went to my desk, gave the signal, and the musicians began.

I knew my score by heart. What, then, was my surprise at hearing, instead of what I expected, some strange sounds which bore no likeness to my opéretta. I could make out the tunes, but the scoring was entirely different from mine. Some inventive local musician had thought proper to compose a new score according to his own ideas!

My first impulse was to leave the rehearsal at once, and to give up all thought of leading the orchestra in the evening. Mdlle. Aimée, however, begged me so hard to stay, representing that I was on the bills, that the public would be angry if I did not appear, that the performance would even be impossible, that I finally allowed myself to be coaxed. I resumed my bow, and gave the signal of attack to my orchestra. What an orchestra! It was small, but wretched. Out of twenty-five musicians eight were pretty good, six were indifferent, and the others decidedly bad.

To guard against all eventualities, I first of all requested a second violin to take a kettle-drum, and I gave him my instructions privately. This was a lucky thought, as will be seen hereafter.

The rehearsal was so deplorable, that when it was over I made new efforts to be excused from leading. It was time lost; I found it impossible to escape from the execution of my music.

"Come what may," I thought, "I have promised to lead two acts. I will lead them, with the help of Providence."

What a performance! You should have heard it. The two clarionets emitted false notes every instant—except, however, when they were needed. In the comic march of the first act I have noted a few bars purposely out of tune, and this always produces an amusing effect. When they had reached this particular passage, the clarionets stopped, and went on merely counting time; the fool who had scored my music had written this piece for the quartette only. At the rehearsal I had begged these gentlemen (the clarionet players) to play, no matter what, in this place, feeling certain that the false notes would come naturally.

But I had reckoned without my host; relying upon their text, the rascals absolutely refused to go on.

"We have pauses to mark; we must mark them; there is nothing written for us."

"But, gentlemen, the false notes you utter when there are no pauses are not written either, and nevertheless you do not spare them."

It was impossible to convince them. As for the hautboy, he played from time to time as he felt inclined; the flute blew when he could; the bassoon slept half the time; the violoncello and double-bass, placed just behind me, skipped note after note, and smuggled in a base of their own fancy. While leading with the right hand, I had at every moment to stop either the bow of the double-bass or that of the violoncello. That was to parry the false notes. The first violinist, an excellent one, was always too hot; the thermometer stood above 100 degrees in the room, and the poor fellow was continually trying to wipe his forehead. I appealed to him in a beseeching tone: "If you forsake me, my friend, we are lost!" He put away his handkerchief mournfully, and took up his instrument; but the flood of false notes kept constantly raising. Happily the first act was drawing to a close.

An enthusiastic success!

I fancied I must be dreaming.

All this was nothing to the second act. Still following my own score, as originally written, I turned to the flute, who should, according to the text, have struck in at this point; but it was the trombone on the right who responded instead.

The two clarionet players had, according to my score, a song in tierce. The local musician had given it to the cornet-à-piston, who played false, and to the bassoon, who was still asleep. At last, and not without much difficulty, we reached the finale. I doubted very much whether we should get through it. The duet between Rose and Bavolet went on after a fashion, but it went on. The finale follows the duet, and as the latter ends in C, I have of course made for the entry of Clorinde, which begins in B major, the modulation in C sharp, E sharp, E. The bass plays the sharp. My little march had been scored by the musician of X——, for the famous clarionets, the hautboy player, who did not play, and the bassoon, who was sleeping more soundly than ever. I made desperate signs to his neighbor, who woke him suddenly. If I had only known, I would have let him alone; for instead of striking the A sharp, he struck up E sharp with all the strength of his lungs. Five notes too high! The unfortunate artist who played Clorinde naturally followed the natural ascension, and also started the melody five notes too high. The orchestra, paying no attention to all these particulars, went on playing five notes too low, and one may imagine the cacophony. I made desperate signs to Clorinde and to the musicians, while the perspiration was streaming from my face. An inspiration from heaven at last came to my aid. I made an energetic and desperate sign to the drummer. He understood me, and a vigorous roll that made the windows rattle—a roll of thirty bars, that lasted until the end of the duet, and which completely drowned, heaven knows, how many false notes. The public certainly never understood why, during a mysterious scene in the middle of the night, that drum was heard so loud and so long; perhaps they took it for a flash of genius on the part of the composer. Such was it, indeed, for it saved the situation. I never think without a cold shudder of the horrors which the rolling of that drum covered up.

After this piece of eccentricity I expected a torrent of abuse from the newspapers, when giving an account of the performance; on the contrary, it was praise, and only praise, which they bestowed upon me for the masterly manner in which I had led.

# CHAPTER XXIII.

### THE FIREMEN OF NEW YORK.

To go to New York and not to see how fires are put out in America would be a most unpardonable neglect. If by chance you should not have an opportunity of witnessing such a sight in the natural course of events, you have only to get into the good graces of my friend, Mr. King, and he will put you in the way of enjoying the sight at your ease, and without any risk either to your own or your neighbor's property.

I was invited to be present at an experiment of this sort, organized specially for my benefit, one evening after my concert at Gilmore's Garden.

I cannot do better on this occasion than to quote the *Figaro*, where my visit is admirably described by M. Bertie-Marriott, the able correspondent sent by M. de Villemessant to America as the representative of his journal.

I think my readers will be thankful if I do not confine myself to the passage concerning the firemen. As there is in the earliest portions of this article a good deal said about me, and as the title of this book compels me at times to speak rather more of myself than I should like, I am happy that another has, in this instance, taken upon himself to give an account of my doings. Here is, then, without further preamble, the article in question:

"NEW YORK, 5*th June*, 1876.

"One engine, that of the railroad, has brought me to Jersey City; another, that of the ferry-boat, has landed me in New York, the 'Empire City' of the continent. Here we were, on board of that vast construction, the ferry-boat, a whole crowd of men, horses, and carriages. All were standing, men and beasts—all anxious to arrive at their destination. It was night, and yet it was evident that all these people were in haste—in haste to take their rest and to get rid of sleep.

For is not sleep so much lost time? To-day drives them towards to-morrow, and to-morrow is for each what yesterday was—business, struggle. Time is money; therefore let none be lost.

"The conversations are curt, and always on business. It would not be an exaggeration to say that out of every hundred words spoken, the word *dollar* is heard seventy-five times. The golden calf has many worshippers, and there is no Moses to overthrow him. To my great astonishment, I hear frequently uttered the well-known name of Offenbach. 'How is this?' I thought. 'Have I been asleep, and been unconsciously carried back to Paris?'

"My neighbor reassures me. I am indeed in New York, and our sympathetic maëstro is there also; so my informant tells me. He leads an orchestra nightly; crowds go to hear him, to see him, to touch him. 'He is a great musician,' adds the Yankee; 'they pay him one thousand dollars a night just to lead the orchestra!'

"That is the whole point for this man-dollar. 'They pay him one thousand dollars!' With what admiration and respect, with what metallic quiver of the voice, he speaks these words: 'They pay him one thousand dollars!'

"For this American it is not that brilliant and sparkling music that will gain his enthusiasm and applause; it is that figure of one thousand dollars a night which gives the value of the master. How could it be otherwise? It is the first word he has heard as a child; it was his first love as a young man; it will be his only passion through life.

"I follow my guide, and, emerging from some badly lighted streets, I come suddenly to an immense covered garden, lit by a thousand colored lights. It is vast, it is splendid; what a crowd! what a lot of pretty women!

"I reach with difficulty the centre of the garden, it is so densely packed. Upon a platform a hundred musicians are waiting, their eyes fixed upon the baton of the leader. There he is himself; and he appears a little nervous under the eager glances of that curious multitude.

"The piece is a polka, composed on board the steamer expressly for the Americans; the fact is known, and the public is therefore pleased. The rhythm is sometimes slow, sometimes rapid, intermingled with songs and laughter; it is brilliant, exciting; and I surprise these people, usually so cold, so preoccupied, and for whom amusement itself is almost a bore, laughing most heartily. Musicians and public are both carried away; thunders of applause are heard; the piece is unanimously encored, and has to be performed over again.

"It is over at last; he comes down, and is kindly permitted to pass. '*Figaro*,' he exclaims, as he sees me—'*Figaro* in New York! This gives me still more pleasure than what you have just seen and heard.'

"Taking me by the arm, he leads me through the crowd, who, from this mark of friendship, must take me for a 'distinguished personage.' How many pretty young ladies would like to hang upon that celebrated arm, that arm which makes one thousand dollars a night!—they look at me positively as if I were robbing them.

"'You must come with me,' said the maëstro. 'I have just been invited to go and see the firemen; and you understand that I am very anxious to see this institution, of which we have heard so much, and of which they are so proud.'

. . . . . . .

"Well, it is wonderful, incredible! Had we not been there ourselves, watch in hand, we would never have believed it; we would have said: Get out, you are a humbug!

"Here is in a few words what we saw:

"One of the chiefs of the Fire Department, Mr. King, accompanied us. 'Name any post you would like to take by surprise!' he said. The Eighteenth street engine-house being close by, Offenbach mentions it, and we direct our steps towards it. Arriving at the door, Mr. King requests us to pay particular attention, and to take out our watches; he then rings a little bell; the door is opened, and we enter. The engine is there, bright and shining; further back, three horses stand in their stalls, ready harnessed. The firemen are asleep upstairs. A gong hangs upon the wall. 'Be careful now, and stand out of the way of the horses,' says Mr. King. And he gives the alarm by striking the gong.

"The three horses are harnessed; twelve men

are there, who climb upon the engine and take hold of the horses; the driver shouts, 'Ready!' 'How long?' asks Mr. King. Six seconds and a half had elapsed since the gong sounded! Without one word, without grumbling, the horses are returned to their stalls, the men go back to their beds. The inspector had the right of seeing if the service was well done; he was satisfied the men had done their duty.

"I confess I had not had time to distinguish anything. I had heard a noise as of distant thunder: it was the men; I had felt the floor shaking dreadfully: it was the horses; I had seen a red glare: it was the furnace of the engine; I had caught a glimpse of a dark form grasping the reins: it was the driver about to call out '*ready;*' but, I repeat, I had had no time to distinguish anything, and yet, as the driver said, all was ready—in six seconds and a half!

"I looked at Offenbach; he was dumb, and still staring, although everything was already in its usual order; his eyes were fixed and vacant as though he were under the influence of a temporary night-mare; he looked dazed, and I fancy I did not look unlike him. Have I succeeded in giving you an idea of this terrific, overwhelming, lightning rapidity? The thought of our French fire-engines crossed my mind, and I felt ashamed.

"'What do you think of it?' asked Mr. King.

"'I have seen many fairy pieces,' said Offenbach, who had recovered the use of speech, 'but never anything to equal this.'

"Mr. King smiled. 'I am going,' he said, 'to show you something better still; come with me.' We followed him; and having reached Madison Square, he stops us in front of a tall pole.

"'I am going to open this box,' he continued, 'and you, maëstro, will press the knob inside, which communicates with six posts or companies like the one we have just left, each stationed at different places—the nearest about one mile, and the furthest about two miles off. Prepare your watches; by pressing the knob, you will give the alarm in these six posts. Are you ready? Press!'

"It was midnight. Many carriages were still circulating through the adjacent streets. All at once, and from all directions, the sound of bells is heard, accompanied by a fearful rumbling noise. The carriages at once drive to one side of the way; the foot passengers stand motionless; on all sides is heard the cry, 'Fire! fire!'

"They arrive at full speed, roaring, hissing, puffing, emitting clouds of smoke and steam. Firemen and engines are on hand. '*Where? Where?*' ask the men. The horses are already unhitched; the hose fast and ready. 'Where? Where?' A sign stops this ardor; each one returns to his post without a word of displeasure or a sign of annoyance.

"'How long?' asked Mr King.

"'Four minutes and a half!'

"Thus, in four minutes and a half, six powerful engines were ready to pour torrents of water on the threatened building; by pressing another knob, six more would have been called; and in the same manner all the engines in the city would have come if necessary.

"Never, as long as I live, will I forget the emotion which I had experienced that night. 'Do you wish to see anything more?' asked Mr. King.

"'No, no, this will do; it is too exciting.'

"And again I cannot help thinking of a fire in Paris; of the senseless shouts of the crowd; of the absurd little machine, with its little buckets; of those hand-engines, arriving always when the evil is already past remedy; of our brave firemen running, full of ardor, it is true, but out of breath, and tired out, before they have commenced their task.

"What a contrast! All this is here, and any one may come and see it. Come, Messrs. Underwriters, come and see for yourselves; you would gain, and so should we, by importing this system into France; your profits would be greater, and our dividends more satisfactory. Come! a little courage, a little effort against routine, and I promise you that your first night in New York will be as well employed as mine. . . . but, alas, you will not come!

"(Signed), BERTIE MARRIOTT."

I will add only two words to the faithful account which the correspondent of the *Figaro* has given of my stupor, on witnessing the astounding agility of these American firemen. I caught them just as the strokes of the gong had started them from their sleep. Nothing more marvellous than to see them slide from their beds, drop into trowsers, which form one piece with their boots, fasten their suspenders, put on their leather helmet, and leap upon their horses— these men, who from sleeping soundly in their beds, are transformed in the twinkling of an eye into wide-awake firemen, dressed and on horseback. It was better than stage fairydom; it was real magic.

## CHAPTER XXIV.

#### BANQUETS, BATON, AND BREVET.

Before leaving New York for Philadelphia I gave a banquet to my orchestra.

Before giving ourselves up to the composition of speeches, and enjoying the excellent *cuisine* of the Brunswick, I received a mark of esteem from my musicians, accompanied by a material souvenir, both of which afforded me much gratification. They came in a body to offer me a leader's baton, which was worthy of a field-marshal. This jewel is made of gutta-percha, imitating ebony, the two ends mounted in gold, an agate set in on one side, and an amethyst on the other. In the middle of the baton is a lyre of massive gold, with my monogram. The musicians presented me at the same time with the following resolutions, printed on white satin:

" At a meeting of the undersigned, members of

the orchestra playing under the direction of Jacques Offenbach, at Gilmore's Garden, in this city, it has been :

"*Resolved*, That, desirous of expressing to our honored leader and friend our earnest and warm appreciation of himself, since we have learnt to know him, it is

"*Resolved*, That we tender him this baton, as a testimonial of our cordial sentiments of respect for his well-deserved reputation, so honorably sustained here ; of our admiration for his genius, his talent, and zeal in our profession, and as a tribute of our affection, which he has won by the excellence of all his relations with us.

"*Resolved*, That his constant courtesy, obliging disposition, amiability, and sincere friendship, for each and all of us, have made him dear to our hearts, and will always render pleasant to us the memory of our connection.

"*Resolved*, That we offer him our sincerest wishes for his prosperity and happiness ; and may a success, even greater, if possible, than in the past, crown his future career."

I thanked them warmly, expressing my gratitude, and assuring them that the excellent recollections I cherished of their talent and of their sympathy would live eternally in my memory.

The following day, which was the day preceding my departure for the Centennial City, I entertained at dinner the literary, artistic, and financial celebrities of the Imperial City.

Here is the account of this dinner, as published in the *Courrier des Etats-Unis*.

### "OFFENBACH'S DINNER.

"Few European artists have been received in New York like the composer of the *Grande Duchesse*. It must be confessed, too, that Jacques Offenbach has doubtless received from the fairies that precious gift, which hitherto had seemed to be the exclusive privilege of twenty-dollar gold pieces: he pleases everybody. The composer's talent may be questioned, but no one can fail to feel kindly towards the man. His cordiality, his modesty, his brilliant wit, always prompt for repartee, yet never departing from the laws of the strictest courtesy, his unpretending affability, acquire for him the friendship of all. He has received here every homage; he has been surrounded with flattering attentions, entertained, serenaded, and honored in every way. In return for all this courtesy, he offered, on Wednesday night, to the press and to a few eminent members of the artistic world, a dinner, or rather a banquet, of which the most skeptical stomachs, if not the hearts, will retain an eternal memory.

"It was in the dining-saloon of the hotel Brunswick that this charming *fête* took place. Representatives of all branches of arts were invited; music, literature, painting, sculpture, and even finance met there around the social board.

"When the exquisite cheer and delicate wines, the enumeration of which would be too long (besides, charity forbid us tantalizing our absent friends to that extent), had raised the spirits of the guests to the proper pitch, the toasts began:

"Offénbach naturally led off, opening the ball in the most attractive, the most humorous, and at the same time the most feeling of all speeches, past, present, future; he drank to the press, the New York press, and especially to the French press, to which he said he owed in a great measure his success and the popularity of his name.

"Mr. Fr. Schwab replied in behalf of the American press, and M. Ch. Villa in that of the French journals. Doctor Ruppaner captivated the attention of his hearers by a brilliant address, expressed in the most elegant terms. Mr. S. Fiske, of the Fifth Avenue Theatre, replied in behalf of the artists. M. Auguste Bartholdi, author of the statue of Lafayette and of "Liberty Enlightening the World," commenced in his turn, and proved that he understood the art of Demosthenes as well as that of Phidias. M. Skalkowsky, member of the Russian Commission at the Exhibition, explained, in a few eloquent words, spoken in the purest French, a few general and generous ideas upon the relations between Europe and America.

"All these orators were vehemently applauded; as to the host, sitting as grave as an Olympian god upon his cloud, yet as gay as an epicurean in the exercise of his functions, he faced everything, replied to every one, and ended by proposing a toast to Francis Kinzler, the organizer of this exquisite and elegantly served supper. It was now day-light, and the guests, seeing the sun about to rise, concluded, with much satisfaction, that they were as virtuous as it is possible to be here below."

The next day I gave my farewell concert in Gilmore's Garden, which on this occasion was crowded to excess. I could see from the stage nothing but a moving sea of heads. My pieces were encored two, and even three times, with desperate enthusiasm.

In vain I put on my coat and hat, descended from the platform, and looked beseechingly at these amiable Yankees; it was of no use. They clapped their hands with frenzy; they knocked with their canes against the chairs; they smashed the benches, until I returned to my stand. Then there was a roar of satisfaction for a moment, after which the most perfect silence prevailed in the hall during the execution of the piece.

At the close of the last piece, my orchestra joined the crowd, and made the ovation more overwhelming still.

I was so overcome that it was with difficulty I could find words to thank these kind friends.

To the deafening hurrahs of the spectators was mingled a joyous blast, spontaneously executed by a number of the musicians; whilst the violinists performed the *ratta* by knocking with their bows upon the backs of their instruments.

In the midst of this manifestation, I received, from the hands of the first violinist, in the name of all his associates, that famous brevet of membership in the association of the musicians of New York which I mentioned at the commencement of these remarks.

I promised then that, before my departure for France, I would give a last concert for the benefit of the association, of which I was henceforth a member.

# CHAPTER XXV.

### FAREWELL NIGHT.

On my return from Niagara I gave the promised concert. The immense placards with which the walls were covered announced to all that I was to appear for the last time. I had never before seen my name under this aspect; the letters were as tall as I am and four times as broad. The American public showed a due appreciation of these splendid bills. Gilmore's Garden was filled with the *élite* of New York society. The moment I appeared I was hailed with cheers, hurrahs, and enthusiastic applause. And they say Americans are a cold-blooded people! I will spare you the particulars of that night, for aside of the fact that I have sworn to speak as little as possible of myself, I must confess that I was so overcome by this unexpected manifestation that I did not very well comprehend what was going on around me.

After the concert, I found with difficulty a few words to repeat, once more, my thanks to my musicians for the valuable assistance they had given me during my visit, expressing the wish, of the sincerity of which they could have no doubt, that the success they so well deserved might continue long after my departure. They thanked me for the performance I had given for the benefit of their association, and made me promise to return to America in the course of two or three years. I promised, as people promise at such times; but, should circumstances permit, I assure you that it would be very pleasant to me to return to Yankee-land and to improve my acquaintance with this marvellous country and with this great people, who showed me a degree of sympathy which will ever remain dear to my memory.

# CHAPTER XXVI.

### HOMEWARD-BOUND.

On the 8th July I sailed on board the *Canadas* which, to my great satisfaction, happened to be ready to leave for France at the same time as myself. Many of my American friends insisted upon escorting me as far as my cabin.

Shall I attempt to express, dear French reader, the joy with which one treads the deck of the vessel that is to take you back to your own country, and to restore you to those who are dearer than the most dazzling success or the most numerous dollars?

Ah! it would have taken a mighty large sum of money to have induced me to leave this vessel! Among the passengers who were returning to France with me was M. de la Forest, the French Consul at New York, who was going on leave of absence for a few months, on account of his health; M. Baknutoff, Secretary of the Russian Legation at Washington, a most distinguished young man, who never allowed the conversation to flag at the captain's table, and from whom I won numerous games of *bezique* to while away the long leisure hours of the passage. We had also two doctors as passengers, Dr. Bastien and Dr. Roussel, who were both ill during the passage, a circumstance which I doubly regretted, as they were both, although Republicans, genuine travellers—that is, men who had seen and read much, and understood life thoroughly.

There was also my excellent friend, M. Bertie-Marriott, correspondent of the *Figaro*, with whom I had the pleasure of talking over the various excursions we had made together in America as well as of discussing the manners and habits of the New World, which I was to sketch after my return home.

I will also mention, while sending them my kindest remembrance, should these lines ever fall under their eyes, M. Glisenkeimer, an American merchant, and one of the gayest of polyglots; M. Schorestene, and Mr. J. White—

the latter a mulatto, who had taken the first prize as violinist at the Paris *Conservatoire.*

The weather was splendid during the whole passage, and there were only three little incidents to note during the trip. The first was at the moment of starting. The vessel, through the carelessness of the pilot, ran against the *Amérique,* another French vessel, which was to start the following week. We cut a deep gash in Captain Pouzolz's ship, and one of our life-boats was crushed. The sinister crash, caused by the collision, made a deep impression upon me. Fortunately, fright was the only harm done.

The second incident was more comic than terrible. One evening, as we were sitting in the saloon, chatting and taking tea, we were surprised to see a Portuguese passenger come in, dressed, or rather undressed, in the costume of a baker at work; the unfortunate man was intoxicated. Fortunately, there were only two or three ladies on board, and, before he had time to commit any excess, the purser took charge of him and led him to his cabin. It seems that he had disposed that evening of a whole dozen bottles of rum.

The third incident is so sad, and yet so ridiculous, that I have decided, after correcting my proofs, to suppress it. Perhaps I may relate it at some future time; but at the present moment I should deem it a want of respect towards the kind and indulgent reader to reveal to him some of the sad details of life at sea.

It was half-past eight when the *Canada*, under a radiant sun, and upon a sea whose surface was as smooth as a mirror, came in sight of the lovely hills of Normandy and entered the harbor of Havre.

To complete my joy, my entire family and many of my friends had been waiting for me for hours, and all my children were waving their handkerchiefs excitedly as they caught sight of me on the deck.

My joy was as great on again seeing my beloved family as my sorrow had been when I had left them. I wept with emotion, and could scarcely forbear throwing myself into the sea to put an end to this agony of seeing there all that was dearest to me in the world, and yet not being able to clasp them to my heart.

An hour later the ship was fast at the dock, and I had become once more Offenbach in France.

THE END.

# 1877. 1877.

# NEW BOOKS

### AND NEW EDITIONS,
RECENTLY ISSUED BY

## G. W. CARLETON & Co., Publishers,
### Madison Square, New York.

─o─

The Publishers, upon receipt of the price in advance, will send any book on this Catalogue by mail, *postage free*, to any part of the United States.

─o─

All books in this list [unless otherwise specified] are handsomely bound in cloth board binding, with gilt backs, suitable for libraries.

─o─

### Mrs. Mary J. Holmes' Works.
| | | | |
|---|---|---|---|
| Tempest and Sunshine............ | $1 50 | Darkness and Daylight.......... | $1 50 |
| English Orphans... ..... ..... | 1 50 | Hugh Worthington............ | 1 50 |
| Homestead on the Hillside..... | 1 50 | Cameron Pride................ | 1 50 |
| 'Lena Rivers..................... | 1 50 | Rose Mather................... | 1 50 |
| Meadow Brook.................. | 1 50 | Ethelyn's Mistake............. | 1 50 |
| Dora Deane...................... | 1 50 | Millbank...................... | 1 50 |
| Cousin Maude.... ............ | 1 50 | Edna Browning............... | 1 50 |
| Marian Grey..................... | 1 50 | West Lawn........(New)........ | 1 50 |
| Edith Lyle........(New)......... | 1 50 | | |

### Marion Harland Works.
| | | | |
|---|---|---|---|
| Alone............................. | $1 50 | Sunnybank..................... | $1 50 |
| Hidden Path...... ............. | 1 50 | Husbands and Homes.......... | 1 50 |
| Moss Side.... ............. | 1 50 | Ruby's Husband.............. | 1 50 |
| Nemesis........................ | 1 50 | Phemie's Temptation........... | 1 50 |
| Miriam ........................ | 1 50 | The Empty Heart... .......... | 1 50 |
| At Last....................... | 1 50 | Jessamine..................... | 1 50 |
| Helen Gardner................. | 1 50 | From My Youth Up........... | 1 50 |
| True as Steel......(New) ....... | 1 50 | My Little Love. ....(New).... | 1 50 |

### Charles Dickens—15 Vols.—"Carleton's Edition."
| | | | |
|---|---|---|---|
| Pickwick, and Catalogue........ | $1 50 | David Copperfield............. | $1 50 |
| Dombey and Son............. .... | 1 50 | Nicholas Nickleby,. .......... . | 1 50 |
| Bleak House.................... | 1 50 | Little Dorrit......... .......... | 1 50 |
| Martin Chuzzlewit..... ....... | 1 50 | Our Mutual Friend.......... ... | 1 50 |
| Barnaby Rudge—Edwin Drood.. | 1 50 | Curiosity Shop—Miscellaneous. | 1 50 |
| Child's England—Miscellaneous. | 1 50 | Sketches by Boz—Hard Times... | 1 50 |
| Oliver Twist—and—The Uncommercial Traveler ..................... | | | 1 50 |
| Great Expectations—and—Pictures of Italy and America................ | | | 1 50 |
| Christmas Books—and—A Tale of Two Cities.................. ... | | | 1 50 |
| Sets of Dickens' Complete Works, in 15 vols.—[elegant half calf binding]. | | | 60 00 |

### Augusta J. Evans' Novels.
| | | | |
|---|---|---|---|
| Beulah.......................... | $1 75 | St. Elmo....... ............ | $2 00 |
| Macaria........................ | 1 75 | Vashti........................ | 2 00 |
| Inez.... ..................... | 1 75 | Infelice...........(New)........ | 2 00 |

## G. W. CARLETON & CO.'S PUBLICATIONS.

### Miriam Coles Harris.
Rutledge .......................... $1 50
Frank Warrington ............... 1 50
Louie's Last Term, etc. ........ 1 50
Richard Vandermarck ........... 1 50
The Sutherlands ............... $1
St. Philip's ..................... 1
Round Hearts, for Children ... 1
A Perfect Adonis. (New) ...... 1

### May Agnes Fleming's Novels.
Guy Earlscourt's Wife ......... $1 75
A Terrible Secret ............... 1 75
Norine's Revenge ............... 1 75
A New Book ..................... 
A Wonderful Woman ........... $1
A Mad Marriage ................ 1
One Night's Mystery ........... 1
Kate Danton. (New) ........... 1

### Grace Mortimer.
The Two Barbaras.—A novel ... $1 50  Bosom Foes. (In press) ...... $1

### Julie P. Smith's Novels.
Widow Goldsmith's Daughter .. $1 75
Chris and Otho .................. 1 75
Ten Old Maids ................... 1 75
His Young Wife. (New) ........ 1 75
The Widower .................... $1
The Married Belle .............. 1
Courting and Farming .......... 1

### Captain Mayne Reid—Illustrated.
The Scalp Hunters ............. $1 50
The Rifle Rangers .............. 1 50
The War Trail .................. 1 50
The Wood Rangers ............. 1 50
The Wild Huntress ............. 1 50
The White Chief ................ $1
The Tiger Hunter ............... 1
The Hunter's Feast ............. 1
Wild Life ....................... 1
Osceola, the Seminole .......... 1

### A. S. Roe's Select Stories.
True to the Last ................ $1 50
The Star and the Cloud ....... 1 50
How Could He Help It? ....... 1 50
A Long Look Ahead ........... $1
I've Been Thinking ............ 1
To Love and to be Loved ...... 1

### Charles Dickens.
Child's History of England.—Carleton's New "*School Edition.*" Illustrated .. $1

### Hand-Books of Society.
Habits of Good Society.—The nice points of taste and good manners ........... $1
Art of Conversation.—For those who wish to be agreeable talkers or listeners .... 1
Arts of Writing, Reading. and Speaking.—For self-improvement ............... 1
New Diamond Edition.—Small size, elegantly bound, 3 volumes in a box ......

### Mrs. Hill's Cook Book.
Mrs. A. P. Hill's New Cookery Book, and family domestic receipts .......... $

### Famous Books—"Carleton's Edition."
Robinson Crusoe.—New 12mo edition, with illustrations by ERNEST GRISET .... $
Swiss Family Robinson.—New 12mo edition, with illustrations by MARCKL ....
The Arabian Nights.—New 12mo edition, with illustrations by DEMORAINE ....
Don Quixote.—New 12mo edition, with illustrations by GUSTAVE DORÉ .........

### Victor Hugo.
Les Miserables.—An English translation from the original French. Octavo ..... $
Les Miserables.—In the Spanish Language. Two volumes, cloth bound .......

### Popular Italian Novels.
Doctor Antonio.—A love story of Italy. By Ruffini ............................. $
Beatrice Cenci.—By Guerrazzi. With a steel engraving from Guido's Picture ...

### M. Michelet's Remarkable Works.
Love (L'amour).—English translation from the original French ............... $
Woman (La Femme).— ..... Do ........ Do ......... Do .......................

### Joaquin Miller.
The One Fair Woman.—A new novel, the scene laid chiefly in Italy ........... 1

### Joseph Rodman Drake.
The Culprit Fay.—The well-known fairy poem, with 100 illustrations .......... 1

### Artemus Ward's Comic Works.
A New Stereotype Edition.—Embracing the whole of his writings, with a Biography of the author, and profusely illustrated by various artists ..............

## G. W. CARLETON & CO.'S PUBLICATIONS. 3

### Josh Billings.
A New Stereotype Edition of the complete writings of Josh Billings. Four vols. in one, with Biography, steel portrait, and 100 comic illustrations........$4 00

### Bessie Turner.
A Woman in the Case.—A new novel, with photographic portrait of author... $1 50

### Wm. P. Talboys.
West India Pickles.—Journal of a Winter Yacht Cruise, with illustrations ... $1 50

### Dr. A. K. Gardner.
Our Children —A Hand-book for the Instruction of Parents and Guardians......$2 00

### C. H. Webb (John Paul).
Parodies and Poems ...........$1 50 | My Vacation.—Sea and Shore.... $1 50

### Livingston Hopkins.
Comic Centennial History of the United States.—Profusely illustrated.....$1 50

### Allan Pinkerton.
The Model Town, etc.......... . $1 50 | A New Book. (In press)........$1 50

### Mrs. M. V. Victor.
Passing the Portal.—A new story.$1 50 | A New Book. (In press)... ...$1 50

### Ernest Renan's French Works.
The Life of Jesus................$1 75 | The Life of St. Paul... .........$1 75
Lives of the Apostles...... ..... 1 75 | The Bible in India.—By Jacolliot..2 00

### Geo. W. Carleton.
Our Artist in Cuba.—Pictures.....$1 50 | Our Artist in Africa. (In press). $1 50
Our Artist in Peru. Do. ..... 1 50 | Our Artist in Mexico. Do. .. 1 50

### Verdant Green.
A racy English college story—with numerous original comic illustrations......$1 50

### Algernon Charles Swinburne.
Laus Veneris, and Other Poems.—An elegant new edition, on tinted paper...$1 50
French Love-Songs —Selected from the best French authors................ 1 50

### Robert Dale Owen.
The Debatable Land Between this World and the Next................$2 00
Threading My Way.—Twenty-five years of Autobiography..... .......... 1 50

### The Game of Whist.
Pole on Whist.—The late English standard work. New enlarged edition.......$1 00

### Mother Goose Set to Music.
Mother Goose Melodies.—With music for singing, and many illustrations... . $1 50

### M. M. Pomeroy ("Brick.")
Sense—(a serious book).............$1 50 | Nonsense—(a comic book)... .....$1 50
Gold-Dust Do. ............. 1 50 | Brick-Dust Do ...... 1 50
Our Saturday Nights............ 1 50 | Home Harmonies (In press).... 1 50

### Celia E. Gardner's Novels.
Stolen Waters—(in verse).........$1 50 | Tested .......... . (in prose).$1 75
Broken Dreams Do. ......... 1 50 | Rich Medway's Two Loves. Do.. 1 75
A New Novel. (In press)....... 1 50 |

### Mrs. N. S. Emerson.
Betsey and I are Out.—Poems...$1 50 | Little Folks' Letters.—Prose.. . $1 50

### Louisa M. Alcott.
Morning Glories—A beautiful child's book, by the author of "Little Women"....$1 50

### Geo. A. Crofutt.
Trans-Continental Tourist from New York to San Francisco.—Illustrated.$1 50

G. W. CARLETON & CO.'S PUBLICATIONS.

## Miscellaneous Works.

Johnny Ludlow.—A collection of entertaining English stories............... $1
Glimpses of the Supernatural.—Facts, Records, and Traditions........... 2
Fanny Fern Memorials.—With a Biography by James Parton................ 2
How to Make Money; and How to Keep It.—By Thomas A. Davies.......... 1
Tales From the Operas.—A collection of Stories based upon the opera plots.... 1
New Nonsense Rhymes.—By W. H. Beckett, with illustrations by C. G. Bush.. 1
Wood's Guide to the City of New York.—Beautifully illustrated.......... 1
The Art of Amusing.—A book of home amusements, with illustrations......... 1
A Book About Lawyers.—A curious and interesting volume. By Jeaffreson.... 2
A Book About Doctors. Do. Do. Do. 2
The Birth and Triumph of Love.—Full of exquisite tinted illustrations...... 1
Progressive Petticoats.—A satirical tale by Robert B. Roosevelt............. 1
Ecce Femina; or, the Woman Zoe.—Cuyler Pine, author "Mary Brandegee." 1
Souvenirs of Travel.—By Madame Octavia Walton Le Vert ................... 2
Woman, Love and Marriage.—A spicy little work by Fred Saunders.......... 1
Shiftless Folks.—A brilliant new novel by Fannie Smith...................... 1
A Woman in Armor.—A powerful new novel by Mary Hartwell.............. 1
The Fall of Man.—A Darwinian satire. Author of "New Gospel of Peace.".... 
The Chronicles of Gotham.—A modern satire. Do. Do. .....
The Story of a Summer.—Journal Leaves by Cecelia Cleveland............. 1
Phemie Frost's Experiences.—By Mrs Ann S. Stephens..................... 1
Bill Arp's Peace Papers.—Full of comic illustrations........................ 1
A Book of Epitaphs.—Amusing, quaint, and curious....(New)............. 1
Ballad of Lord Bateman.—With illustrations by Cruikshank, (paper).......... 
The Yachtman's Primer.—For amateur sailors. T. R. Warren, (paper)....... 
Rural Architecture.—By M. Field. With plans and illustrations............. 2
What I Know of Farming.—By Horace Greeley............................. 1
Transformation Scenes in the United States.—By Hiram Fuller......... 1
Marguerite's Journal.—Story for girls. Introduction by author "R.ledge."... 1
Kingsbury Sketches.—Pine Grove doings, by John H. Kingsbury. Illustrated.. 1

## Miscellaneous Novels.

| | | | | |
|---|---|---|---|---|
| Led Astray —By Octave Feuillet.. | $1 75 | Saint Leger.—Richard B. Kimball. | | $1 |
| She Loved Him Madly.—Borys.. | 1 75 | Was He Successful ?........Do. | | 1 |
| Through Thick and Thin.—Mery. | 1 75 | Undercurrents of Wall St. Do. | | 1 |
| So Fair Yet False.—Chavette..... | 1 75 | Romance of Student Life....Do. | | 1 |
| A Fatal Passion.—Bomard........ | 1 75 | Life in San Domingo.........Do. | | 1 |
| Manfred.—F. D. Guerazzi.......... | 1 75 | Henry Powers, Banker ......Do. | | 1 |
| Seen and Unseen...... ........ .. | 1 50 | To-Day... ....... ....... ..Do. | | 1 |
| Purple and Fine Linen.—Fawcett.. | 1 75 | Bessie Wilmerton.—Westcott..... | | 1 |
| Asses' Ears................. Do. | 1 75 | Cachet.—Mrs. M. J. R. Hamilton... | | 1 |
| A Charming Widow.—Macquoid. | 1 75 | Romance of Railroad.—Smith.. ... | | 1 |
| True to Him Ever.—By F. W. R.. | 1 50 | Fairfax.—John Esten Cooke..... | | 1 |
| The Forgiving Kiss.—By M. Loth. | 1 75 | Hilt to Hilt. Do. ........ | | 1 |
| Loyal Unto Death................ | 1 75 | Out of the Foam. Do. ........ | | 1 |
| Kenneth, My King.—S. A. Brock,. | 1 75 | Hammer and Rapier.Do. ........ | | 1 |
| Heart Hungry.—M. J.Westmoreland | 1 75 | Warwick.—By M. T. Walworth.... | | 1 |
| Clifford Troupe. Do. | 1 75 | Lulu. Do. ... | | 1 |
| Silcott Mill.—Mrs. Deslonde...... | 1 75 | Hotspur. Do. .... | | 1 |
| Ebon and Gold.—C. E. McIlvain.. | 1 50 | Stormcliff. Do. .... | | 1 |
| Robert Greathouse.—J. F. Swift.. | 2 00 | Delaplaine. Do. ... | | 1 |
| Charette..... ................ 1 | 1 50 | Beverly, Do. ... | | 1 |

## Miscellaneous Works.

| | | | |
|---|---|---|---|
| Beldazzle's Bachelor Studies.... | $1 00 | Northern Ballads.—Anders n..... | $1 |
| Little Wanderers.—Illustrated.... | 1 50 | O. C. Kerr Papers.—4 vols. in 1.... | 2 |
| Genesis Disclosed.—T. A. Davies. | 1 50 | Victor Hugo.—His Life.......... | 2 |
| Commodore Rollingpin's Log... | 1 50 | Beauty is Power............... | 1 |
| Brazen Gates.—A juvenile........ | 1 50 | Sandwiches.—Artemus Ward...... | |
| Antidote to Gates Ajar.......... | 25 | Widow Spriggins.—Widow Bedott. | 1 |
| The Snoblace Ball............... | 25 | Squibob Papers.—John Phœnix,... | 1 |

www.ingramcontent.com/pod-product-compliance
Lightning Source LLC
Chambersburg PA
CBHW020816230426
43666CB00007B/1034